DECOUPAGE
OLD AND NEW

DECOUPAGE OLD AND NEW

By Elyse Sommer

Watson-Guptill Publications / New York

Published 1971 in New York by Watson-Guptill Publications,
a division of Billboard Publications, Inc.,
165 West 46 Street, New York, N. Y.

Manufactured in Japan.

ISBN 0-8230-1316-2

Library of Congress Catalog Card Number: 74-157650

First Printing, 1971

*To Mike, Paul, and Joellen—
my severest and most encouraging critics*

ACKNOWLEDGMENTS

I wish to express my sincerest appreciation to the following artists for allowing me to borrow and photograph their work for this book. Alice Balterman, for Figures 61, 62, 108, and 134, which she supplied; Carl Greenberg, Artist's Haven, Cedarhurst, Long Island, for Figure 57; Helen Gluskin, for Figure 8; Janet Landau, for Figures 5, 7, 72, and 130; Winnie Lynn, for Figure 110; Helen Russell, for Figure 36; Joellen Sommer, for Figure 115; and to the students of Turtle Hook Junior High School, Uniondale, Long Island, and their teacher, Selma Feld, for Figures 63, 65, and 66. Figures 135 and 136 were used courtesy of Stair & Co., photographs by Helga Photo Studio and Ramond Fortt, respectively.

All photographs of the author's work by Burton Stuttman.

CONTENTS

Figure 1. A handsome humidor decorated with a combination of ready-colored and hand-colored designs. The top of the box is done with a replica of an Early American painting, and colored reproductions of American state flags fit perfectly around the lid. Both reproductions were received in the mail. To complete the patriotic theme, large eagles from a black and white gift-wrap paper were colored to go with the red, blue, gold, and brown tones of the other designs. (See Color Plate 10.)

1

PAINT WITH YOUR SCISSORS

The dictionary defines decoupage as "to cut out" and that is exactly what you do: cut out a picture or parts of several pictures and combine them into a pleasing design, using any surface in need of decoration as your canvas.

Unlike collage, decoupage utilizes only paper designs and, unless special techniques are used, sinks them beneath many coats of varnish so that the final look and feel are those of a fine enamel. While decoupage is the perfect hobby for those who cannot draw a line, it does require perseverance. You have to have the patience to be a finder of materials, the patience to redefine these materials, and, finally, the patience to integrate surface and background into one piece.

Cutting out pictures! Decorating surfaces! You might wonder whether this is really creative. Is it art as well as craft?

The answers to these questions depend entirely upon you, the decoupeur. If you merely cut out a picture and transfer it to a surface of matching dimensions, coating it hastily with a few protective coats of varnish, the result is neither art nor craft, but merely artsy-craftsy. If, however, you learn to look at existing designs with an inventive eye and you use your decoupage skills of cutting, coloring, and finishing to carry out what you envision, then the result is indeed both art and craft. Like many dedicated modern craftsmen, you will be helping to keep a fine old craft alive in an age overrun with mass-manufactured gadgetry.

Facsimile Editions of Prints

In response to the public's interest in the history of art and architecture, many publishers have produced facsimile editions of engravings and woodcuts. These are perfect for decoupage because of their subject matter, design, and quality of paper.

Thus, the same pictures which inspired the eighteenth-century decoupeur are available to you today. For example, Jean Pillement's gay fantasy flowers, animals, and Chinoiserie (scenes in the Chinese manner) are available as individual prints from crafts suppliers, or as part of a facsimile edition of a book called *Ladies' Amusement*.

This book was first published in 1760 by Robert Sayer, an Englishman. It contained the first collection of the prints of Pillement and other outstanding designers and was printed in response to the popularity of decoupage among ladies of leisure in France and England. There are only a few original editions of *Ladies' Amusement* in existence, including one at the Metropolitan Museum of Art in New York and another at the Victoria and Albert Museum in London. Obviously, even if more of these originals were available, they would be too valuable to cut up.

Another facsimile, a large paperback, costing just a few dollars, offers hundreds and hundreds of woodcuts by the famous eighteenth-century English engraver, Thomas Bewick. There are many such treasures available. These are all uncolored materials and thus ideal for fine decoupage which always involves hand-coloring prints.

Other Sources for Prints

For those who do not want to color, or who wish to combine ready-colored and hand-colored materials, there are many choices and possibilities. There are children's book illustrations by artists ranging from nineteenth-century favorites, such as Kate Greenaway and Randolph Caldecott, to outstanding living artists, like Tasha Tudor and Maurice Sendak. These prints are often available in inexpensive editions; many are in color, some are in combinations of color and black and white.

The Suppliers List at the back of the book will give the names of some of the publishers, book dealers, and print suppliers who have catalogs available from which you can order by mail. In fact, every material needed to make any of the projects described in this book can either be bought in a local paint, hardware, or hobby shop, and/or by mail.

Of course, one of the most pleasurable aspects of decoupage is searching out your own design materials in book shops—both old and new—book sales and fairs, flea markets, and print shops. Your local stationery and gift store can be a veritable treasure trove. Most gift wrap designs are already colored and many are too "cartoony" and two-dimensional to warrant the designing and crafting effort involved in good decoupage. However, the quality and artistic range of these papers are constantly improving and expanding. Black and white designs are also being offered more and more frequently. A word of advice: if you do find a particularly usable gift wrap paper, buy enough of it, for the manufacturers are always replacing old papers with new ones and they do not keep stock of their "back issues." Stationery and bridge pads, like the gift wraps, should be used with discrimination. If they are not usable as an over-all design, they often provide good border materials which can be combined with hand-colored prints and thus serve as a coloring guide. Finally, there is your own mailbox. Once you become a decoupeur, even so-called "junk" mail is fraught with possibilities (Figure 1).

Choosing Designs

It matters very little whether you work with prints of the French Chinoiserie type or with more contemporary materials. But try to choose things of intrinsic artistic worth. Interesting shading and modeling on prints make better decoupage material than flat two-dimensional drawings. Pictures which lend themselves to combination with other prints are better than something which you transfer intact to another surface like a decal. Flat, nonglossy paper surfaces are desirable; in fact, they are a must for hand coloring since glossy papers do not take color well. You will also find that the glossy surfaces such as those in monthlies like *McCall's* and *Good Housekeeping* have a tendency to bleed when wet.

The completely glossless newsprint paper used for newpapers and many Sunday supplements is the cheapest paper made and it is very pulpy and not likely to take well to pencils or to varnish. As soon as the varnish touches it, the print on the backside of the paper is likely to show through, obliterating the design you want. In some cases, the paper might actually disintegrate.

Choosing Materials

A general interest in art and art history might lead you to decoupage because of the wealth of available material to cut, color, and design. If this is so, there are many excellent and varied materials which will allow you to achieve truly craftsmanlike results. In fact, there are so many finishes and finishing aids used in decoupage that the beginner might be tempted to go out and overstock and overspend, depending upon art supplies more than art sensibility to insure perfect results. Save your money until you have practiced on something small and inexpensive. Stick to the very basic supplies and beware of fancy finishes and trimmings. However, you need not go overboard in the opposite direction. To do good cutting, you do need a crisp, good quality scissors. Do not use an old box for decoupage to be thrifty; if the shape is awkward and unwieldy, decoupage is not going to take away its basic gracelessness. If, however, the shape is well proportioned, decoupage will enhance those good proportions and you will be spurred on to an interesting layout (Figures 2 and 3).

Choosing a Finish

While a fine piece of decoupage is worth the time involved in applying many, many coats of antique varnish and waiting twenty-four hours between applications, there may be times when you will want to try a modern finish which builds up and dries faster. For example, you might receive a short notice invitation to visit someone to whom you want to give a personalized handmade gift. At such times it's good to be familiar with some of these new, fast finishes. Some are very good, some inferior, so that you must experiment and test. However, even when you opt for the short-cut finish, don't feel that you must rush through the cutting and creating process. Anything worth doing, large or small, antique or modern, is worth doing well. Thus, while you may not have the time, inclination, or space to do decoupage on a grand scale, approach it with an attitude of crea-

Figure 2. *This box was found in a junk store. It had an ugly veneer covering which required a bit of elbow grease to remove. The attractive design surface and well-shaped sides with their soft apron effects and the feet made it well worth salvaging. The box was painted white with a gold-leaf effect. The Grecian figures are in soft antique reds and greens and are color coordinated with the scrolls. Note how the top border is repeated around the sides, achieving a nice over-all unity. (See Color Plate 3.)*

Figure 3. *The box shown in Figure 2 was designed with these two prints which came from different sources. Note how the curved portion of the border print (left) had to be combined to form an enclosing oval for the figures (right).*

Figure 4. A handmade papier-mâché box, painted a bright yellow, with black and white prints arranged to suggest an intermission at the opera. A lining of music paper carries through the mood of the opera theme.

Figure 5. An old iron, painted black and decorated with yellow and green scrolls and tiny angels, becomes a conversation piece.

tive craftsmanship. Any craft undertaken in a truly inventive and adventurous mood can offer limitless opportunities for self-expression.

Choosing a Surface

In addition to the joys of turning plain objects into *objets d'art*, decoupage offers a marvelous opportunity to explore and utilize other crafts. Instead of searching for something to go with a certain scissor painting, the imaginative decoupeur will eventually look for ways to make his own surfaces to decorate. Papier-mâché and ceramics make wonderful surfaces. With the cost of crafts materials rising along with everything else, the economic advantage to be gained from making your own surfaces cannot be discounted.

This process of searching out new ways to use an art form is tremendously challenging. A walk along the beach may result in the idea for rock decoupage. A visit to an art exhibit may start the idea for mosaic decoupage. Since photographs are so much a part of our modern lives, the possibility of using photos in combination with traditional decoupage opens up still another avenue of exploration.

This experimental approach carries over to materials. The old-time master craftsmen would probably have wanted to explore materials such as polymer gloss and silicone sealer if they had been commercially available. In this book, because it *is* a twentieth-century book, I have combined the old with the new. Obviously, there will be some methods which might not quite fit in with a traditionalist's approach to decoupage.

I think traditional decoupage is beautiful and exciting. You can remain within the accepted concept of decorating surfaces and continue to learn and grow artistically. But, like many of my students, you may want to take that extra step into the wide and wonderful world of crafts in general.

The surface you create when you enter into this "total crafts" phase may not be as perfect as the wooden box you buy in a shop, but the satisfaction to be gained from going all the way is likely to more than compensate for these slight imperfections. (See Figure 4.) Designing ideas will change and grow; new methods and materials will suggest themselves. Decoupage is indeed an art which is totally open-ended. You can explore it as deeply as you wish, guided by artistic inclinations.

Figure 6. An old metal tin is painted a soft blue and decorated with Godey ladies and flowers. Note how the flower design on top is carried through on the sides of the box. The ladies and flowers are colored in soft blues and lavenders. (See Color Plate 8 for the other side of the box.)

Figure 7. A mirror is brightened with flowers from a book on flowers. The background is antique white.

Figure 8. A small traveling case, the leatherette backing and rusty hinges removed, was painted black and covered with black and white designs. Even the hinges are paper, hand drawn with black pencil-holes to resemble nails, an example of a craftsman's ingenuity.

Figure 9. This unusual frame of corn husks, painted in very dark, antique brownish gold seemed perfect for a Gothic-style picture. The scene is made up from numerous sources, carefully hand colored. The castles are from old theatrical prints, the figures from a book on the Renaissance. The background panel is Masonite painted with hand-tinted deep gold gesso.

Figure 10. *An elegant box designed on top, front, and back, across each side which opens up when the inside drawers fold out, and inside the top and front lids. The designs came from five different sources of similar mood. One floral design was used to coordinate all the parts. The use of reds, greens, golds, and oranges was coordinated throughout. The gold border around the top served a double purpose: to keep the top design in a central position and to conceal little chips at the edge.*

Figure 11. *This box was designed especially for a friend who collects presidential memorabilia. The pictures of George and Martha Washington, from a book of old playing cards, combined very well with the border design. The box was painted antique white and became very old and mellow-looking under varnish. This old look is especially pleasing to collectors and antiquers.*

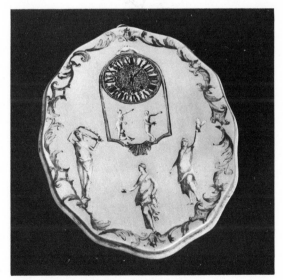

Figure 12. *The clock design serves as a focal point in this plaque. The figures in the clock were taken from an alphabet of tiny human figures. The lovebirds nesting at the top were added for balance and interest. The Grecian figures encircled by a scroll provide good "gaze motion." Note how heads and arms are placed so that the viewer's eye is guided to take in the entire scene.*

Figure 13. *A pair of black candlesticks with the designs left uncolored, except for the mellowing produced by varnish.*

2

TECHNIQUES

The ability to select prints and redefine them into an individual artistic statement cannot really be taught. It is largely a process of developing an awareness of the colors and shapes all around you and of the ideas you can get from shops and shop windows, from museums, and from the pages of books and magazines. If you have the urge to create something distinctive and beautiful with decoupage, you'll soon find out which prints you prefer and how to arrange them for your own purposes.

Choosing the Design

Your chief consideration in planning a good composition is to unify the background of your design with the surface on which you are working. They don't have to "match," but they should be related in mood and color (Figure 10).

To think up design ideas, try to come up with a theme. The use to which your decoupage will be put will help in theme selection. Are you making a gift for someone and, if so, what are his special interests? (See Figure 11.) A screen done around a theme of children (Figure 133) called for an accompanying motif. Gaily colored flowers and butterflies seemed to have a natural affinity for these central figures. A patriotic theme seemed most appropriate to decorate an old humidor. (See Figure 1.)

Planning the Composition

Once you have chosen your design, there follows the process of planning your composition. There really is no great mystery or difficulty about assembling your design into a pleasing layout. Your own taste will guide you instinctively. Actually, it is rather like casting a play. The producer picks the stars and then adds the rest of the cast. In the same way, you will pick out your most conspicuous element and place it in a focal position with the minor details strategically grouped around it. Keep in mind the "gaze motion" created by your design. This means its optical effect, the way the viewer's eye is led to focus on the various elements of the design. An enclosing scroll, a figure facing in a certain direction are easy and subtle means of directing the viewer's attention.

The craft techniques of decoupage can be mastered by anyone with the will and the patience. Once you learn to master these skills, you can undertake anything from simple projects to large "heirloom" pieces. We will consider these techniques in the order they are applied.

Coloring

Since there are so many colored prints available, this step may be optional. Designs in black and white turn an interesting shade of ivory under varnish and may be left to more or less color themselves. (See Figure 13.) However, hand coloring does add depth and dimension to your work, heightens your own artistic perception and, of course, gives you full control in terms of achieving exactly the effect you wish. To quote the heroine of Muriel Spark's *The Prime of Miss Jean Brodie*, hand-colored decoupage is "the crème de la crème."

Choosing Your Coloring Materials

Here are some of the materials you will want to have on hand.

Pencils. You should have about twelve to fifteen oil-based colored pencils. Derwent, Eagle Prisma-

Aabcdefghilmnopqrstruxyz.

1

2

4

3

Figure 14. *A number of different prints were needed to design a box with as many dimensions as the one shown on Figure 10. While different prints were used, everything combined in mood. An italic alphabet (above) was used to write the words "truth" and "beauty" on the inside lid cartouches. (1) This design was used as a focal point to pull the various elements together through the box. The complete scroll was used on the box top and a large portion was used on the sides. The flower containers were used as part of the front and back design. (2) Designs used as part of the box top and front lid design. (3) Designs used on the inside of the front lid. (4) Designs used inside of top lid.*

tics, and Venus are the most popular brands and are widely available. Do not buy pastel sticks or pencils. The oil-based colored pencils are somewhat softer, can be blended easily, and will not smudge. A very workable selection of colors would include two shades of each primary color (red, yellow, blue), each secondary color (violet, orange, green), plus terra cotta, black, white, and flesh. (See Figure 14.) These basic shades can be blended and combined to give you a full color range.

Pencil sharpener. It is important to work with well-pointed pencils. Therefore, a good pencil sharpener is a necessity.

Pink eraser. Use this to lighten some of the very dark spots of your print before you start coloring and, of course, when you change your mind.

Clear plastic spray. This is useful for many phases of decoupage. A coat of clear spray is the easiest way to seal in colors and prevent them from running or bleeding when you apply your varnish. Another alternative is a brush-on sealer, either commercially prepared, or your own solution of half shellac, half distilled alcohol. This last is excellent, keeps well in a sealed jar, and is inexpensive. However, most of my students prefer the ease and speed of the canned spray. (See the Demonstration on coloring at the end of the chapter.)

How to Color

As soon as you start coloring you will understand why the paper you use should have a flat rather than a glossy finish. A shiny surface does not "take" the pencil colors. Whatever color *does* adhere does not come through in clear tones and what's more, the minute you spray or varnish, it is likely to fade away. You will also realize that the dark spots in your prints can actually work as a guide to interesting shade and texture.

Start by filling in the dark spots and the dark outlines with the darkest shades and then work outward towards the lighter areas with your lighter color. (See the Demonstration on coloring at the end of chapter.) Use your white pencil to blend the dark and light shades together. Do not smear it, but press down firmly. You will see that this blending action erases the crayon-y look and gives a painted finish. You could use a very light shade of the color as a blender instead of white: light pink for shades of red, light blue for blues, etc. In addition to using the shaded spots to guide your choice of shades, use them to guide the direction

of your pencil strokes. *Never, never* go across lines. *Always* go in the direction of the shading lines.

Follow the entire contour of what you are outlining. A rose, for example, would be done with round strokes. This is part of the over-all effort to achieve depth and contour. Your cutting will reinforce this effect also.

While you can apply one color over another to achieve deeper, brighter shades, do leave some spots uncolored. These are your highlight areas. Look at any painting and you will see that the artist always adds a dab of white or yellow in strategic areas or leaves the area untouched so the white background shows through. It is a good idea to emphasize white highlights by going over them with a white pencil. This will make them shine through the layers of varnish you will be adding.

Choice of Colors

Your choice of colors is, of course, up to you. If you feel uncertain as you start out, pick two or three shades of your favorite color. For example, red, red-orange, and orange—or yellow, yellow-green, and green. The colors facing each other on the color wheel always make for good combinations. (See Figure 14.) For example, red and green, blue and orange, or yellow and violet. You might find that copying the colors of a finished print is a good way to begin.

Clothing and furniture displays, magazines, and illustrated books can furnish inspiration for color combinations. A visit to an art gallery to study the way painters use color can be equally instructive. You will discover that an almost immediate sense of increased appreciation and awareness of good art is one of the many "bonuses" you will enjoy when you study decoupage.

Coloring Exercises

Here are some coloring exercises which should be helpful. I will be referring to the print in the coloring demonstration at the end of the chapter, *Step 2*, but you could use any print offering similar shading and contours.

Using One Color

Take a dark and a lighter shade of one color, perhaps a dark green and a lighter green. These two pencils plus white are all you will need. Now, take your darker pencil and sharpen it well. First,

go over all the dark outlines of the flower branches. Next, take your lighter green and fill in the inside portions, using firm, even strokes. Keep your strokes going in the same direction, rather than back and forth. Then, take your white pencil and blend the dark and light. Do not smear or smudge or you will obliterate your colors.

If you feel some of your shaded areas are now too light, take your dark pencil once again and reaccent your outlines. You can go over your penciling in this way not only to reaccent, but to deepen colors. The idea is to intensify rather than to try to use pressure and do it all in one heavy application. This last method would give you a smeary, unattractive look, rather than the depth of shading you want.

Using Several Colors

In this exercise you will use a few more colors and concentrate on working with the contour of a print. The curved flowers and leaves in our print are ideal for this exercise. Your two shades of green can be used for the leaves, but try some additional colors for the flower. Perhaps a deep red and a pinkish red, plus yellow for the center and to add accents of light, would be the best colors to use.

To do the leaves, start with your dark green pencil and go over the outline and the dark shaded lines at the center of the leaf. Note how these lines curve and be sure you curve your lines out with them. Again, do not run your pencil back and forth to cover these shaded lines. Instead, start each stroke at the center and make curved strokes outward. You will be using a series of curved strokes from the center of the leaf to the right edge of the leaf. Then you will go back to the center and curve your pencil in the opposite direction, from center towards left edge.

Now take your lighter green pencil and use the same technique for the light unshaded areas. Leave a dot here and there uncovered for the light unshaded areas. Leave a dot here and there uncovered for a highlight. Use your yellow pencil to go over these little spots. Use your white pencil to blend from the dark to the light areas. If necessary, go back over the dark areas with the dark pencil.

The flower could be colored in much the same way as the leaf. Use the dark red pencil to go over the black outlines and the shaded lines. Again, be sure to follow the curve of these shaded lines. If you go across or against these lines, you will lose

Figure 15. Four little scenes are effectively unified into frames and scroll, beautifully fitting the title The Four Eras of Life. *Since the scenes were found in old* Godey's Book *magazines, this seemed an apt over-all title.*

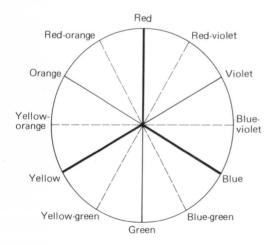

Figure 16. Here is a color wheel. The darkest lines indicate the primary colors, red, yellow, and blue. From these basic colors all other colors are obtained. The solid lines indicate the secondary colors, violet, orange, and green. These secondary colors are obtained by combining those primaries adjacent to each other: red and yellow combined to achieve the secondary color, orange; yellow and blue combine to achieve the secondary color, green; blue and red combine to achieve violet.

the distinctive shading quality that makes hand coloring so attractive.

When all the shaded areas are finished, use the lighter pencil to fill in the white areas, again going with the curve of the petals and again leaving a dash here and there uncolored. Either the yellow or the white pencil can be used to go over the highlight spots. In fact, the yellow pencil can be used very firmly over the center portions of the flower.

You will find that you can now hand color any flower. However, remember that the fun of decoupage coloring is that you can follow nature's palette or select your own; creating fantasy flowers can be most exciting.

Using a Range of Colors

A complete group of colors would include: flesh, white, terra cotta, red, deep yellow, a lighter yellow, two shades of blue, and two shades of green. I find that coloring figures is a good way to discover how to play various colors against one another. All the varied colored clothes should first be given a note of uniformity. Start with your terra cotta pencil and apply this color to all the shaded areas. When this part of the project is completed, you can use your greens and blues in various combinations. If you do not have a flesh-colored pencil for the faces and hands, you can use a soft pink or red and bring down the skin tones with yellow.

Since the world is made up of people with a variety of skin colors, you might try soft browns overlaid with flesh, or pink and yellow, with touches of terra cotta. You will find you can achieve skin colors for all types of people. Be sure to accent the eyes and the shading around the cheeks, mouths, and hands. Black brings out the features. Green and yellow can be used to tone down too pink faces.

I like to apply eyeshadow and rouge to the people I am coloring, especially ladies and little girls. Hair colors are achieved with shades of brown, yellow, terra cotta, and purple. Terra cotta plus red will give you a henna redhead, terra cotta plus yellow, a red-blonde. Brown hair can be highlighted nicely with a touch of crimson. Your white pencil will again serve to blend your various shades together, but remember to blend from dark to light.

Sealing Your Colors

If you were to paste down your print without first sealing in the colors, some of these colors would run at the first contact with varnish, thus smudging the background. To avoid this, always seal your colors as soon as you have finished coloring and *before* you start cutting. A coat of clear plastic spray will do the job, although a brush-on sealer is just as effective. Do not drench your print in spray or the liquid will wash off the coloring. Hold your print at arm's length, away from the can. Apply a light coat, moving the hand holding the spray in a circular motion. The idea is to spray out a light mist, rather than a heavy coating.

To keep your spray applicator from getting clogged (and this applies to any spray you use anywhere, be it a household, cosmetic, or paint spray), turn your can upside down when you are done and push your button until no more spray will come out. The first time you do this, you will feel you are wasting a whole lot of spray. However, you will see that the spray stops coming out almost instantly, and this release of air pressure actually saves your material in the long run.

Special Coloring Trick

For a quick and easy way to blend the crayoned look of your pencils to a smooth watercolor finish, wrap a facial tissue or paper napkin around the tip of the lightest color pencil used. Press down and rub back and forth. (See the Demonstration on blending colors at the end of the chapter.) In a very small design where colors might smudge up into a face, it is best to stick to the white pencil as a blender since it offers firmer control.

Thinning Your Prints

If you want your design to paste down smoothly, and if you want your paper to be somewhat thinner, now is the time to razor thin your design. This step might save five or six coats of varnishing, if not more. (See the Demonstration on thinning prints at the end of the chapter.)

Cut away all the portions of the print except those which you have colored and planned to use. Lay your print, face down, on a firm solid base such as a heavy piece of cardboard, or a thickly folded newspaper. Now take a single-edged razor blade and shave about ten strokes from the center out to the edge. You will see shavings of paper coming loose. By stroking the razor from the center to the edge you are helping to contour your edges downward which will help them to lie flat.

Another reason you might want to razor your print besides thinning is to avoid worrying about a design on the back of a page showing through when you paste and varnish. Some marvelous books have designs printed on both sides of the page. By razor thinning the backside you will be taking off the back-page design and thus any likelihood of this second print showing through is eliminated.

Since most paper is made in layers, all but the thinnest papers can be peeled by soaking or sponging off layers. However, this is a risky business: the danger of ripping the paper is tremendous. Even if you do get several layers of paper peeled off without tears or nicks, you may have peeled off so much paper that the print is too fragile for you to work with. The only time I recommend wet peeling is when you are working with something heavy like a postcard. In this case, you can safely soak your paper in cool water for a minute. After soaking, place the paper face down on a hard surface, pat it dry, and then pick it up so that you can try to grab hold of a loosened corner with your fingernail. The back layer should come off all in one piece.

In preparing a very large project with many cutouts, razor thinning is too time consuming. It would be more advisable to count on doing extra varnishing, if you are working on this type of project.

Cutting

Although anyone can be a scissor wizard, this is the one decoupage skill which seems to intimidate most beginners. New students will invariably ask, "How can I possibly handle those delicate lines, or get into those tight little spots? " One cutting session and they *think* they can do it; a second cutting session, and they *are* doing it!

You will need one pair of sharp cuticle scissors about three inches long. Straight borders can be cut with ordinary, small embroidery scissors. (See the Demonstration on cutting prints, *Step 1,* at the end of the chapter.)

The first thing you do is to cut away excess portions of paper from around your print so that your hands will have as little as possible to hold. Hold your cuticle scissors so that the tips point away from the print you are cutting. The hand holding the paper will be doing as much work as the one manipulating the scissors. The idea is to keep feeding the paper into the base of the scis-

sors' blades. In other words, you are actually cutting with the blade base, not with the tips. You will use the tips only when cutting into a corner or a very tight space.

Remember to keep the scissors pointed outward, away from the direction in which you are cutting! While you are practicing, exaggerate the feeding of paper into blade. You should feel as if your paper is seesawing back and forth; your cutting edge will have tiny notches. This type of edge will lie and paste down more tightly and securely.

Cutting Exercises

Take a blank sheet of paper and cut out really exaggerated zigzags; you will be making big scallopy outlines. If you move your paper with less pronounced movements, your zigzag edges will get smaller and less pronounced. Keep doing this until you can create an edge which resembles a finely serrated knife.

Take some magazines and practice cutting out designs. You will find that when you work with materials which you know you will be throwing away, you will be more relaxed about cutting into things. Stick to cutting out these throwaway designs until your confidence is thoroughly built up. Remember, too, that you and you alone are the designer. If you should accidentally cut off a little flower or a leaf, so what? Who said you *had* to have that leaf in your design? You can always substitute something else.

Suppose you do accidentally cut through an integral portion of a design, does that mean you must throw the whole thing away? In practically all cases, the answer is "no." If you paste carefully, a design put down in sections will look all of a piece. In fact, when working with a large design, many decoupeurs find it preferable to purposely cut their large scroll, or whatever, into sections for ease in handling during both cutting and pasting.

Three Cutting Tricks

To get the best results, when you are cutting out your prints, be sure to follow these rules.

(1) Cut away the inside portions of your design first so that you will always have something to hold onto. (See the Demonstration on cutting prints, *Step 2,* at the end of this chapter.)

(2) When cutting into tiny openings, use your scissors tip to stab a hole from the top. Then cut

in, still with the point, from underneath. Keep cutting from underneath, using the tips, as long as the space is tight. Once you learn to get in from underneath like this, no cutting job will seem insurmountable.

(3) Draw yourself a "security line" whenever things look too thin to handle. Be sure the pencil that you use for thickening is sharpened to a fine point and matches the rest of the design in color. Sometimes you can even draw a line where none exists to give yourself a connecting link. (See the Demonstration on cutting prints, *Steps 3 and 4*, at the end of the chapter.)

Gluing

"Bubbles, bubbles, toil and troubles! " Keep this counsel in mind when you are tempted to rush through this process. The same beginners who tend to be intimidated by fine cutting, have a tendency to oversimplify gluing. After all, everyone has glued things! Yet, while gluing is, indeed, easy enough, it is crucial to take the proper precautions. If one spot of your print is not covered with glue, the minute you start to varnish, this spot will pop up and an air pocket will form.

Gluing Materials

Here are the materials you will need for gluing.

Glue. Use the white water-soluble type.

A small wide-necked, seal-top container. Transfer the glue, which most likely comes in a pointy-topped plastic glue bottle, into a container into which you can dip your fingers or a brush.

Glycerine. This is a drugstore item. A few drops added to a small container of glue will make the adhesive more manageable because it will help to retard the setting time. Glue can also be thinned with a little water.

A bowl. This should be filled with water and used frequently for cleaning your fingers.

A sponge. Use a damp sponge as a combination clean-up and tamper.

A dry, clean cloth. Use this for drying your design after it has been glued down. Paper towels are also good.

Wax paper. This will be used to prevent the print from sticking to other surfaces when it is being pressed down on the surface to be used.

A small roller (or a spoon). This is to be used as a tool for pressing down prints.

Clear plastic spray. This is the final sealer for your glued-down prints.

Gluing Techniques

Before gluing, gather your materials on a table covered with newspaper. Apply glue sparingly either to the background or to the back of the design. Use your fingers or a small brush as an applicator. (See the Demonstration on gluing, *Steps 1 and 2*, at the end of the chapter.)

Put your design on a clean surface with the unglued side face up. Then, dip your fingers into water and dry them thoroughly. This step is important even if it sounds like a lot of fuss. If you don't stop to clean your hands, a delicate design can stick to your fingers and rip when you try to paste it down. If you don't dry your hands thoroughly, water can get between your glued print and surface, preventing its permanent adhesion.

With your hands clean and dry, you are now ready to place the print down where you want it. You will have about a minute to move it around, if you are not satisfied with its placement. Now, take your sponge, moistened but almost dry, and use it to gently tap down your design as you squeeze out any excess glue. You can use the tip of the sponge to clean away any of the excess glue; this minimizes later cleanup. (See the Demonstration on gluing, *Step 2*, at the end of the chapter.)

Next, tap your design gently with a dry, clean cloth or a piece of paper toweling. Make sure everything is down tight and dry.

Now, to make sure your design will adhere firmly, place a piece of wax paper over your glued-down, dry design and with a small wallpaper roller or the back of a spoon, press down for a really firm adhesion. The wax paper will protect your print from being damaged by your pressing tool but, in spite of the paper, go easy. (See the Demonstration on gluing, *Step 3*, at the end of the chapter.)

Finally, remove the wax paper and let everything dry for at least six hours; overnight is preferable.

When everything is dry, recheck your pasting job. Test the edges with your fingernails. Use a toothpick to slip a dot of glue under any portions which might have become loose. If any part of the center portion of the design seems loose, you are bound to have a bubble in your print as soon as you varnish. Now is the time to prevent this problem. Take a single-edged razor blade and make a slit right in the center of the part that is loose. Then, take a toothpick, add a little glue to one end, and slip it into the unglued area. Tap the area down with your dampened, almost dry, sponge, and allow it to dry some more.

To clean up, take a cotton swab, or the tip of your sponge, and dip it in warm water. Use this to clean away any glue spots, either on top of, or around, your design. Don't *wash* it, just dab it clean.

A final, very thin film of clear plastic spray will seal your colors and produce a nice clean surface, but this is not essential.

Varnishing

An absolutely perfect piece of decoupage—finished with an antique varnish (which takes twenty-four hours to dry thoroughly, though it will be dry to the touch before that), hand-rubbed with wet and dry sandpapers, steel-wooled, and finally waxed— has a buttery patina which makes people tend to gasp in awe and delighted disbelief when they first see and feel it. There are faster drying varnishes available, and these are being improved upon all the time, but do not expect miracles. A varnish which builds up very fast and thickly, and requires just a few coatings, is unlikely to give the results of a fine semi-gloss furniture varnish. This particular varnish has been used for decoupage and fine furniture finishing for many years. It is still available in all paint and hardware stores, and continues to be most acceptable.

With so many new finishes available, it is good to remember that the slower drying varnishes tend to be more durable than the faster drying ones. Lacquer-based finishes can be applied every hour, allowing you to finish a project very fast. However, these finishes are non-yellowing. A varnish will mellow and yellow your colors, an effect which most decoupeurs find quite pleasing. Lacquer-based finishes are also more likely to crack under extreme temperature changes. Thus, lacquer-based finishes are recommended more for jewelry, ceramics, and small projects in general; they are not for fine wood surfaces.

You will probably want to experiment with a variety of materials, but I would suggest that you do your starting projects as if you were doing a grand piano for a museum: hand-colored and antique varnished. Whatever finish you use, *never, never, never* mix different finishes, or brands of the same kind of finish. If a lacquer-based finish is used over antique varnish, it can cause disintegration. Products marked Decoupage Finish, instant, or one-hour drying are almost always lacquer-based.

Varnishing Materials

Here is a list of the materials you will need.

Antique varnish (semi-gloss). This is the best varnish for a fine finish.

Seal-top jars. Transfer varnish into this type of jar to prevent deterioration. The less varnish is exposed to air, the better.

Labels. Use labels to mark your jars. Since jars of varnish should be stored in the refrigerator to prevent the varnish from getting gummy, this will prevent confusion. Varnish tends to look like iced tea or apple juice, so beware. Mark your jars carefully and prominently. Put on a poison sign if there are children who cannot read in the house. If you do not want to transfer your varnish, or you dislike the idea of cluttering up your refrigerator, buy the smallest can available. Then, be sure to seal it tight after each use, and hammer the can shut! Store it upside down so that any scum which forms will remain at the bottom.

Wooden coffee stirrers. Use these to stir the varnish before each use. Popsicle sticks will serve this purpose too.

Varnish brush. I find inexpensive household brushes most satisfactory. Small ½" brushes are best for small items. I rarely use anything wider than a 1" brush. Foam brushes, again in the household-hardware rather than art supply category, avoid the problem of hair marks and although they are featured as throwaway brushes, I have used them over and over again.

Foam dishmop. Using strips of foam is one of the easiest and least messy ways to varnish without any brush. Just cut pieces of foam from an inexpensive (25 cents) foam dishmop into small strips, which will be discarded after use. One dishmop will provide dozens of usable strips. (See the Demonstration on varnishing at the end of the chapter.)

A word of caution about foam: it holds much more liquid than a bristle brush. You have to dip into varnish very lightly and apply the varnish with a light touch.

Brush cleaner. A water-based brush cleaner will preserve the life of the cheapest brush indefinitely. However, the brush should be cleaned always with soap and water *after* immersion in the brush cleaner. When your brush is thoroughly clean, wrap it in a paper towel or tin foil to keep it free of dust.

A detergent low in phosphate content may also be used as a brush cleaner.

Many of my students do not clean their brushes at all; they wrap them in tin foil and store them in the freezer between varnish applications. This keeps the brush moist and usable.

Blue oil tint. If you want to avoid the yellowing caused by repeated applications of antique varnish, put a drop or two—but no more—of blue oil tint, such as Universal tinting, into your varnish and stir. This is available in a tube from any paint or hardware store.

Other Finishes

Lacquer-type finishes must be cleaned off the brush with lacquer thinner. When using lacquer finishes, the brush should be kept standing in the thinner between applications. This keeps the brush soft and serves to make the lacquer, which is heavy and dries almost as it touches a surface, more manageable. When you are ready to apply the lacquer, just rub the brush, which has been in the thinner, against the sides of the jar and dip the still damp applicator into the lacquer. (See the Demonstration on lacquer finishing at the end of the chapter.)

How To Varnish

Always stir your varnish before using; do this gently with a small stick. *Never* shake the jar instead of stirring.

First, dip your brush into the varnish—not all the way in, just the tip. Let the excess drip back into the jar. (See the Demonstration on varnishing, *Step 2*, at the end of the chapter.)

Now apply the varnish with smooth, even strokes. Start at the center of the piece so that the heaviest application of varnish is deposited there. Stroke very, very lightly at the edges where the varnish tends to build up. Most beginners tend to

let the varnish cake up around the edges. If you do get varnish ridges, they can be scraped off with a razor or with your fingernail. However, be careful not to scrape too close to the design.

Avoiding Varnishing Problems

Here are some suggestions to help you avoid problems during varnishing.

Always inspect your piece carefully before you apply your new coat of varnish. What you will be looking for will be brush hairs and varnish runs. Varnish runs look like tears running down a cheek and they are the result of too much varnish carelessly applied. You will also be looking for dust or dirt which might have settled into the wet varnish and, at the very beginning, for design edges which might have picked up. All these problems can be remedied fairly easily if spotted early enough. But they loom larger and larger, and often get beyond repair, if you allow them to go uncorrected.

A glued edge which has become unglued after one or two coats of varnish can be fixed quite easily. Just take a toothpick and scrape away any varnish which has been trapped underneath the print. Then, take the other side of the toothpick and use it to slip a dab of glue underneath the loosened edge. Tap down with your dampened sponge, and allow to dry overnight before varnishing again.

If any dust or dirt or brush hairs have become embedded in your varnish, or if your piece has accidentally dropped out of your hand, the best time to remedy the damage is while the varnish is still damp. Stop varnishing, even if you are in the middle of an application. Dip a clean rag into mineral spirits (turpentine would be too strong and might damage the prints) and wash off the whole layer of varnish. Allow your piece to dry and varnish it again the next day.

As for varnish runs, they can be gently sanded out with a small piece of No. 400 wet and dry sandpaper. Dip the sandpaper in water, and then rub the offending area with a circular motion. Clean up and proceed with your varnishing. Remember, the best time to get rid of these marks is when they develop!

Give your wet pieces plenty of space in between coats of varnish. Use inverted paper cups, empty Coke bottles, plastic containers, and lids as stands. Hang anything which can be hung on wires. This helps to prevent varnish from caking around edges or different pieces from sticking together. (See the

Demonstration on drying at the end of the chapter.)

When you are varnishing, always work in a clean, dry place with a good light. If your workroom tends to get damp during rainy weather, skip varnishing on those days.

Apply at least twenty layers of varnish and make sure your edges can no longer be felt before you sand. Fifteen coats of varnish is the minimum application before you even consider sanding. Some decoupeurs have given their fine pieces as many as forty coats of varnish. However, in these cases sanding should not be left until the end. It should be started after about twenty coats. Then repeat the sanding and rubbing process after every ten coats, until you are satisfied.

Sanding and Rubbing

There are no tricks to rubbing, just elbow grease. However, if you do not sandpaper until your designs are really and truly sunk in, you will be rubbing just once. Should your surface develop a lot of little bumps, which do have a tendency to crop up if you apply varnish with a heavy hand, then it would be a good idea to start the rubbing process somewhat earlier and repeat several times.

The purpose of sandpapering is to level your edges so that the paper design and the background are of a piece. The steel-wooling finishes off where the sandpapering began and also erases unsightly marks. The wax serves as a protective coating and gives patina.

Sanding and Rubbing Materials

Here are the sanding and rubbing materials you will need. (See the Demonstration at the end of the chapter.)

Wet and dry sandpaper. Available in all hardware stores, it is black on the abrasive or rubbing side, and tan on the back. The tan side is marked several times with numbers showing the degree of abrasiveness. You will need a sheet of No. 320 or No. 360, a sheet of No. 400, and a sheet of No. 600.

No. 0000 steel wool. Available in most hardware stores, this is used to smooth after sanding.

Paste wax. Any good quality can be used according to the company's instructions.

A bowl of water. This should be filled with a water and soap flake paste.

Sponge and dry cloths. To be used for cleaning and drying.

Sanding Procedures

Cut your wet and dry sandpaper into strips about 1" wide and fold the strips up so that you have a surface of about 2". Try to cut the strips so that each one has its identifying number on the back. This will enable you to keep your various grades of papers easily identified. You will be using these strips over and over again, until they lose their abrasiveness.

Make a paste out of soap flakes and water. The soap flakes cut down the harshness of the sandpaper and protect the surface from getting scratched up. Dip your sponge into this solution and thoroughly wet down the surface to be sanded. It is a good idea to work on a table covered with lots of newspapers which will absorb some of the water and soap which you are likely to spill.

Take your No. 320 or No. 360 sandpaper, the harshest of the three grades you will use, and start sanding. Follow your sanding motions with your fingers so that you can actually feel what you are doing. Most decoupeurs going through this step for the first time are simply terrified that they will damage their prints. If you've done your varnishing properly and sufficiently, these fears should go unfounded. Of course, you should remember that you are not scrubbing a filthy kitchen floor and if you are a particularly strong and heavy-armed person, remember not to scrub rather than rub. (See the Demonstration on sanding, *Steps 1 and 2*, at the end of the chapter.)

Knowing what to do *just in case* might calm your fears, so rest assured that even if you do rub through to a print, all is not lost. If this happens, stop rubbing immediately and dry your surface. Then get a colored pencil close to the color of the damaged spot, but a bit darker. Wet the tip of the pencil with your tongue and gently fill in the damaged spot. Now you will have to take some giant steps backwards. Instead of continuing your sanding, go back to varnishing and apply about five coats. When you do go back to sanding, go more gently and circumspectly around the previously damaged spot.

After you have sanded your piece with the No. 360 or No. 320 paper, wet down your surface some more and repeat the same procedure with No. 400 paper. When you have achieved as much smoothness as possible with No. 400, go to the

No. 600 which is very smooth and does the job.

In the event that you are sanding before your designs are sunk into at least twenty coats of varnish—perhaps because you want to get rid of surface bumps before they build up—start with the No. 400 rather than the No. 360 or No. 320, and use only No. 400 and No. 600.

Now, wash down your surface once again. This time, dry it thoroughly with a clean cloth. You will see some moiré patterned marks in the surface. Don't worry about this. The next step will erase all these marks.

Rubbing Procedures

Tear off a small piece of No. 0000 steel wool and rub all over the design in circular motions. You should now be concentrating on the spots remaining bumpy or raised by the sandpaper. At the same time, you will be erasing the marks in the background. This is an important and time-consuming step. Be sure your surface is dry when you use steel wool. (See the Demonstration on sanding, *Step 3*, at the end of the chapter.)

When you have steel-wooled the entire area, wash it once again with soapy water. You will feel the soft and marvelous patina taking shape under your hand as you buff the surface dry.

If you are not fully satisfied with your finish at this point, or you feel your edges could be just a little more sunk in, apply two more coats of varnish. Repeat the steel-wooling but do *not* sandpa-per. Wash and dry the newly coated surface.

Waxing

Most paste wax manufacturers recommend that a damp cloth be dipped into the wax and rubbed over the surface with a circular motion. The wax finish can then be buffed up with a clean, lint-free cloth. Some decoupeurs like to add a dab of their favorite perfume or cologne to the damp waxing cloth!

Since paste wax not only gives your decoupage a marvelous gloss but serves as a protective sealer, it is a good idea to repeat the wax application several times within the first two weeks after completion. You should then regularly wax your piece every four months or so, just as you would fine furniture.

If you ever find that you have to do more work on your piece, the wax finish must be removed. Varnish will not adhere to a wax surface. In a very humid climate, for example, design edges might pop up a little after a year or two. Also, pitmarks might form as a result of some glue or dampness not drying out at the time your design was first glued and varnished. To repair the piece, remove the wax finish with your No. 0000 steel wool. Then wet the surface down and rub it with your No. 400 sandpaper. Dry and steel-wool again. Apply two to six coats of varnish, depending upon your needs. Finally, steel-wool again and rewax. Hopefully, you will never need this advice.

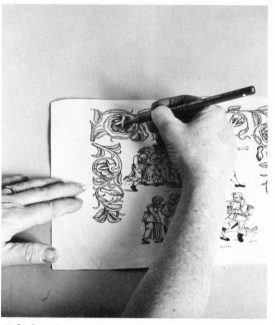

Coloring. Step 1. All the materials needed for coloring: pencils, eraser, sharpener, and clear plastic spray to seal in the colors.

Coloring. Step 2. Start coloring in the dark, shaded areas of your print first.

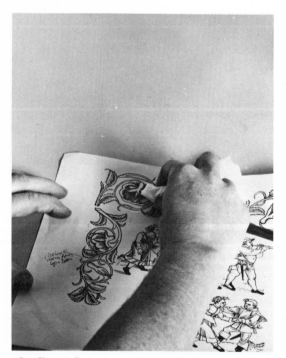

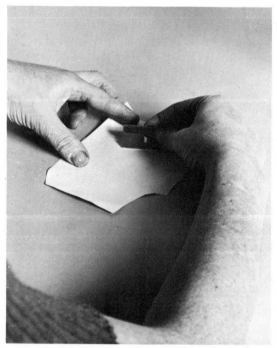

Blending Colors. A special trick for blending pencil colors is to wrap a tissue around the tip of the last and lightest pencil used and work this tissue-covered pencil across the colored surface.

Thinning Prints. A print can be thinned with a single-edged razor blade.

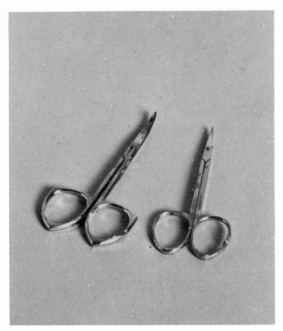

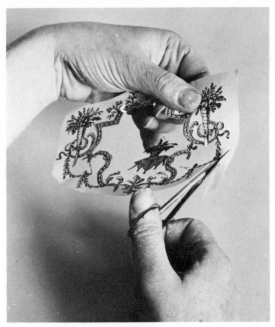

Cutting Prints. Step 1. Decoupage scissors should have a curved tip. Size depends upon your own hands. The important thing is a curved, crisp cutting blade.

Cutting Prints. Step 2. Always cut away excess material so that your hand holding the print to be cut has a minimum to hold. Once you start cutting out your print, work at the inside portions first so that you will always have something to hold on to.

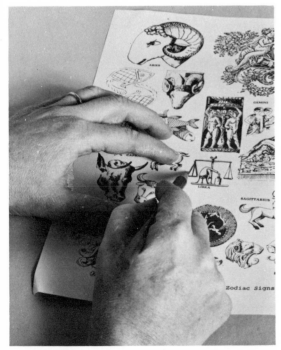

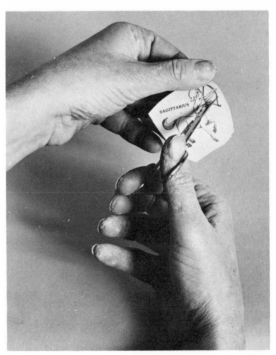

Cutting Prints. Step 3. Very thin lines should be thickened with a matching colored pencil before cutting. These "security lines" prevent thin lines, like the scale of this figure, from coming apart.

Cutting Prints. Step 4. A very tight spot is best attacked by stabbing in from the top, using your scissors points.

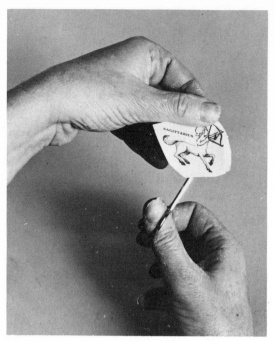

Cutting Prints. *Step 5. Once you've stabbed into a tight spot from the top, come in from the bottom to do your actual cutting. Keep using your point until you have enough room to work comfortably with your blades.*

Gluing. *Step 1. The materials for gluing: water, a sponge, clean rags, wax paper, and a roller. The glue may be applied with your fingers as shown, or with a brush, directly to the print or to the background.*

Gluing. *Step 2. A damp, almost dry, sponge is used to tap down the print and squeeze out any excess glue.*

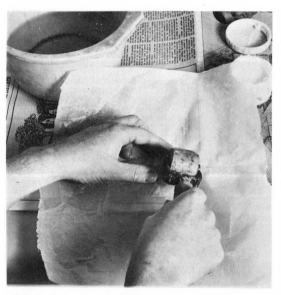

Gluing. *Step 3. After the print is down tight and thoroughly dry, a piece of wax paper may be placed over the print for protection, and a roller, or other pressing tool, used to reinforce its adhesion.*

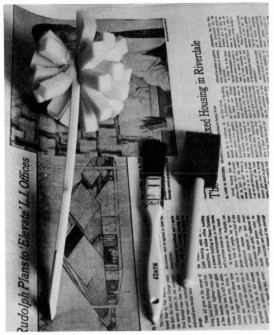

Varnishing. *Step 1. A varnish brush may be an inexpensive household bristle brush, a foam brush, or even bits of foam cut from a dishmop.*

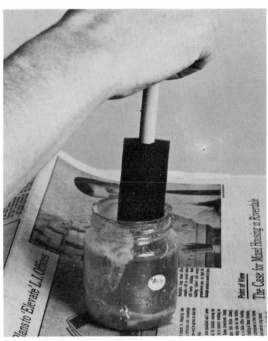

Varnishing. *Step 2. Dip only the tip of your brush into varnish, and let the excess drip back into the jar before applying to your surface.*

Lacquer Finishing. *Lacquer-based finishes require lacquer thinner to clean them off brushes. It is best to keep the brush standing in a jar of lacquer thinner in between applications—do not wipe off all the thinner before dipping into the finish.*

Drying. *Allow your decoupage pieces to dry freely. Raise plaques and boxes up on cans and jars. Let hinged boxes rest open and free. Hang anything that can be hung. Paper cups make excellent props for small boxes.*

Sanding. *Step 1. Have all your equipment for sanding at hand before you begin: your three grades of wet and dry sandpaper, a bowl of soapy water to help prevent scratch marks and keep your sanding surface sopping wet, a sponge, a clean dry cloth, and No. 0000 steel wool.*

Sanding. *Step 2. Be sure your surface is sopping wet during the sanding.*

Sanding. *Step 3. Use your most abrasive (No. 320 or No. 360) wet and dry sandpaper first. Then tear off small pieces of your No. 0000 steel wool and when the surface is absolutely dry, rub it with circular motions.*

3

STARTING PROJECTS

Decoupage may be done on just about any type of surface. It is particularly beautiful on wood. The ivorylike finish of the varnished and rubbed design enhances and enriches any wood's texture. Painted grounds gain a luminous sheen. An inexpensive teak stain takes on the richness and luster of expensive mahogany.

Any simple wooden box or plaque would make a fine starting project. Actually, anything can be used as long as it is not so big that you will become discouraged. Remember, inevitable beginner's mistakes will look larger than life on a large surface. I speak from experience. My first project was a giant screen and for years, every time I walked through my dining room, each error in design, color, and workmanship seemed to shout "I told you so." But, before I discuss some specific starting projects with you, a word about the materials you will be working on.

Preparing Your Backgrounds

If you work with unfinished wooden crafts items, you will be working with raw wood which has open pores. An ordinary oil- or water-based paint will sink into these pores and, unless you seal them off, numerous coats of paint will be necessary. To seal the pores, give your wood a coat of clear plastic spray or a coat of brush-on sealer such as a 50/50 shellac-alcohol mixture. If you use acrylic paints, a sealer is unnecessary; opaque acrylic colors cover any surface beautifully, often with just one coat.

One of the best ways to close the open pores in your wood is to give it a thin base coating of acrylic gesso. This product is available in any paint supply store. It is a white, milky substance, the consistency of thick cream. Painters use acrylic gesso to seal their canvases, and it is an excellent wood sealer. You can use any type of paint as a second coat over the dried base coat of gesso, but do not mix oil colors into the gesso itself. Water-based materials can be mixed only with other water-based materials so beware of trying to *mix* the water-based acrylic gesso with oil paints.

Painting With Gesso

Gesso is well worth trying out as a sealer *and* paint. A base coat, plus another coat, gives a beautiful, milky white base, not only on wood but also on metal, glass, and ceramics. I like to tint my gesso with the watercolors that come in tubes. By doing this, I have obtained lovely and original shades of baby blue, deep gold, and soft pink. If you do decide to try this method of mixing your own gesso, make just a small amount of the mixture, no more than the size of a small baby food jar. Always label it carefully, specifying the exact amount and shade of color used. In this way you can vary the formula or repeat it at a later date.

Your background can be painted with any brushes; inexpensive household brushes, either bristle or foam, are suitable for paints. *Never* mix your varnish and paintbrushes. Use the paintbrushes for paint only, the varnish for varnish, the lacquer for lacquer, etc. If you like spray paints, it is perfectly all right to use them, but I find them expensive and prefer the control offered by the brush-on paints.

Sanding

Most crafts items are sanded down fairly smoothly, but it is always a good idea to lightly sand your surface with regular, medium-grade sandpaper. If

Figure 17. *A metal tin was covered with striped paper to eliminate the need to treat the surface with a rust preventer. The stripes against the black and white figure are very attractive. The roses which decorate the top portion of the box are a good color complement for the green stripes.*

Figure 18. *The music paper background of this plaque gives the effect of having the musicians step right out of the music. The papered part of the plaque is raised. The edges were painted and covered with a garland of flowers. Notice how much is happening in this design. (See Color Plate 1.)*

you are working with a box which has a fitted lid, be sure the fit is quite loose before you paint. If the fit is tight, sand until it is loose. Since paint tends to expand wood, a really tight fit will jam up after painting.

When you are working with old wood, it may be necessary to remove old finishes and to do considerable sanding and cleaning before you can apply fresh paint. If you are going to work extensively with things in need of repair and refinishing, I would like to suggest the following helpful books: *The Furniture Doctor* by George Grotz and *With Love and Elbow Grease* by Elizabeth Lowry Browning.

In the case of metal surfaces, I recommend using a coat of rust retarder unless the item is brand new and specifically identified as being rust treated. Old rust spots must be sanded and washed off. Some of the rust retarders are now available in colors so that, like gesso, you can use them as a rust retarder-paint combination. A coat of clear plastic spray or brush-on sealer should be applied to the surface when it has been painted and before any cutouts are applied.

Papering Your Background

Since decoupage is a paper art, you may sidestep the whole problem of sanding and painting by actually papering your background. There are so many beautiful papers available in art and gift shops that your range of background colors and textures can be as complete as any paint palette. When using a paper instead of a painted ground, unattractive old veneers and nicks can be left in the wood.

If you are papering over a large area, it is probably better to use wallpaper paste. This is a wheat powder that you mix with water to a creamy consistency. It is very inexpensive and available in any paint or hardware store. Use a small roller to roll the paper smooth for small projects, and a large roller or a kitchen rolling pin for large surfaces. Be sure to press out any paste wrinkles when you are covering a surface in this way.

Of course, when you are working with pins or small plaques, a paper background is a matter of taste more than a timesaver. Sometimes, the paper serves to integrate background and design. You can see this in designs featuring musical figures (Figures 18 and 19). Now, we shall discuss some good starting projects.

A Pin or Pendant

These are the easiest, least expensive, and most versatile starting projects. The O-P Craft Company (see Suppliers List) sells very smoothly finished buttons from 1½" to 2½" in diameter. If you specify that you want them without holes, you have the perfect base for a collar pin, or, if you attach a hanging hook, for a pendant, or, if you put them on a piece of velvet inside a frame, a charming addition to a wall grouping. (See Figures 19, 20, 21, 22, and 23). Here are some suggestions to help you in this project.

Decorating a Pin

Some of the buttons may have a slight bump in the center which should be sanded down with ordinary medium-grade sandpaper before you paint or stain.

If you plan to use your button as a pin, you will need a jewelry finding known as a pinback (see Suppliers List, jewelry findings). Even for the small buttons get at least a 1" pinback. Tiny pinbacks do not "sit" right when you put the pin on.

The pinbacks may be attached before or after you finish designing and varnishing the pin. I prefer to attach my findings first. It gives you something to hold onto during varnishing, and makes it easy to hang the pin during the drying time between applications of varnish. Whether you attach your pinback first or later, be sure to place it correctly so that it will "fit" properly when you wear the pin. A little more than halfway from the top is the best placement. (See the Demonstration on decorating a pin at the end of the chapter.)

Decorating a Pendant

If you want to wear your pin as a pendant, place a small picture hook right on top of the pinback. Most hardware stores carry these lightweight little hooks. The hanging or ring part folds over and there are little prongs meant to be hammered into the back of the picture. However, I simply hammer these prongs flat so that my "pendant hook" can be attached with cement.

You could also make a pendant by drilling a hole about 1/8" from the top and inserting a large jump ring—a jewelry finding easily bent open and shut with eyebrow tweezers—through this hole. You can then pull a necklace chain, ribbon, or leather thong through the ring.

The design possibilities for these simple little round shapes are limitless. Again, initials are one possibility so look around for really decorative initials and try to find some design motifs to add to the initial (Figure 23). You will be amazed how much you can do in the way of creating small scenes. Anything you do on a large scale can be attempted and carried out in miniature.

Coasters

For your second project, why not find out whether it is really true that decoupage can turn ordinary objects into *objets d'art*. Every town has dime stores and gift stores which carry inexpensive wooden coasters. These are usually about 3" in diameter. One side has a smooth, inexpensive teak finish; the other is indented to hold a glass. The indentation is framed in teak and backed with cork or plastic. Usually, the coasters are sold in sets of four or six, and they may have a little wooden stand on which the coasters are stacked when not in use. A set of these coasters could be turned into a group of charming plaques. The coaster stand can be used as a paper-napkin holder. (See Figures 24 and 25.) You can use these items "as is," letting the varnish and finishing enrich the texture and patina of the teak stain, or you can paint without any need to sand or pretreat.

Plaques

To turn the coasters into plaques, you use the original underside for your design and fill in the indented part as a backing. This is done quite simply by cutting out a circle of corrugated paper, of the weight used in grocery cartons, to fit the indented portion of the coaster. Glue it in. Then cut a circle to cover the entire coaster either out of a piece of felt or attractive gift wrap and glue that in place. You can use any sort of glue-on picture hook. When finished, your coaster has the back of any well-framed picture (Figure 26). (See the Demonstration on decorating a coaster at the end of the chapter.)

So far we have discussed projects which involve only one decorated surface. From the button pin you can easily go on to larger plaques and panels. You are now on the road to looking at things with a new eye, an eye which will become more and more trained to adapt a variety of shapes for a variety of artistic purposes.

Figure 19. Paper is once again used to integrate design and background. A pin like this is a most appropriate gift for any music lover.

Figure 20. A variation on the personalized initial is a design which includes someone's birthstone, flower, or, as in this pin, a zodiac sign. This handsome, softly colored Aquarius is set against a bright red background.

Figure 21. A small pin can tell as full a story as a larger plaque if you choose and plan your designs carefully. Here, within a surface of just 1½", we have a figure enclosed in a scroll. In addition to being decorative, the angel carries a message. The paper he holds in his right hand was blank in the original print. In this instance, the word "love" was colored in. Any word symbolizing love, friendship, and other ideas could easily have been substituted.

Figure 22. Another pin designed around a special interest. Something as contemporary in theme as this calls for contemporary designs. The ski figure was taken from a ski map. The various road signs were taken from a gift-wrap paper. They add a touch of humor to the design.

Figure 23. *Initials always make good and very personal designs. A good designer will look for interesting initials and add unique touches, such as the face which adds a special note to this initial E.*

Figure 24. *This is the stand in which the six coasters were originally packed. It is now a perfect napkin or letter holder. The other side of the stand has a little boy within the same border design.*

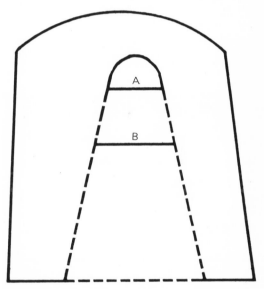

Figure 26. *This diagram shows how to cut the easel with the over-all size of the frame to which it will be attached. The bottom portions should touch the bottom of the frame. There should be a half an inch border between the easel top and the top edge of the frame, and between the easel sides and the sides of the frame. To make the frame, cut through the part marked by the broken line. This is the back part of the easel, which will be pushed outward as a stand. Then bend, but do not cut, at the line marked A in order to push out the leg. Next bend at the line marked B. You will attach the easel by gluing from the B line to the top edge of the easel.*

Figure 25. *When designing plaques in pairs, there should be some unity in the designs of each. These coasters were turned into plaques, and the top and bottom scrolls and the birds establish a sense of unity between them.*

Figure 27. Here is a finished trinket box. The background is painted a soft blue. The flowers on top of the box slope down gently with just two touches of trompe l'oeil. The ladies wandering all around the sides of the box, stand on the side lip. Each figure had to be cut through after it was pasted in order to open the box.

Figure 28. Another way to design the step-by-step trinket box. Instead of having the side designs run through the opening, they were chosen to fit the bottom part of the box. A chain of gold paper braid hides the opening.

Figure 29. A box to hold a roll of stamps is another good starting project. Note the appropriateness of the border design on which the alphabet letters rest. The postal motif of this border is carried through on the top of the box, serving as a ledge for books, a globe, and a bird.

Figure 30. Another small box which could be used for stamps, paper clips, or other small items. The little boy riding the dog is a design from an old school primer. Notice how the border materials are coordinated all around. The colors are brilliant yellows and green against stark white.

Decorating a Box

We will be working with a small box which will require us to think of two surfaces when designing: the top and the sides. Boxes are beautiful in their own right and seem to come in almost limitless numbers of shapes and sizes. Once you can master the design and crafts problems posed by a box, it is only a matter of time, practice, and patience until you can master larger pieces of furniture.

Your first step will be to choose a shape which will appeal to you. The round box meets all the qualities suitable for decoupage. It has good lines, emphasized by a graceful lip around the bottom and a gently sloped top lid. This curved top lends itself to a variety of designs, and even offers the possibility of letting a lid design lap over across the sides. For instance, a flower could be arranged so that it seems to be falling over in the manner of a *trompe l'oeil* or fool-the-eye design. The side could be treated with border materials such as simple narrow scrolls or gold paper braid designs, but is also large enough to accommodate small figures or objects (Figures 27 and 28). The shape would fit into any decor, and the inside proportions are large enough to hold jewelry, paper clips, hair pins, coins, buttons, medallions, and a variety of other odds and ends which are kept in boxes. (See the Demonstration on decorating a box, *Step 1*, at the end of the chapter.)

Preparing the Box

Once you've chosen your box, prepare it by sanding the wood until it is smooth. Clean off the sandpaper shavings with a rag dipped in distilled alcohol. Use sandpaper abrasive enough to really sand down the rim of the lid and the bottom inner rim. The box top must fit loosely to allow for the paint. If you plan to use a wood stain instead of paint, you need not allow for swelling of the wood. Paint or stain your box. (See the Demonstration on decorating a box, *Step 2*, at the end of the chapter.)

It is a good idea to have your designs planned and colored before you paint your box so that the background and design colors are coordinated. If you want to see what your design will look like before you actually paste it down, use bits of an adhesive known by a variety of trade names such as Stick-It, Plasti-Tak, etc. (See the Demonstration on decorating a box, *Step 3,* at the end of the chapter.)

Once you are satisfied with your design, glue everything down very carefully. Cut with a razor any designs which overlap the box lid. (See the Demonstration on decorating a box, *Step 4*, at the end of the chapter.) Varnish until all your designs have sunk in—at least twenty coats even for a little box like this. Sand with your three grades of wet and dry sandpaper, steel wool, and wax. (For finished designs, see Figures 31, 32, 33, and 34.)

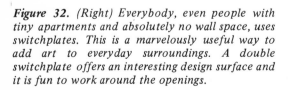

Figure 31. (Above) Salt and pepper shakers become collector's items when decorated with decoupage. The top of one is painted black to indicate pepper. Since this is the sort of thing used as a matched pair, the designs are the same on both.

Figure 32. (Right) Everybody, even people with tiny apartments and absolutely no wall space, uses switchplates. This is a marvelously useful way to add art to everyday surroundings. A double switchplate offers an interesting design surface and it is fun to work around the openings.

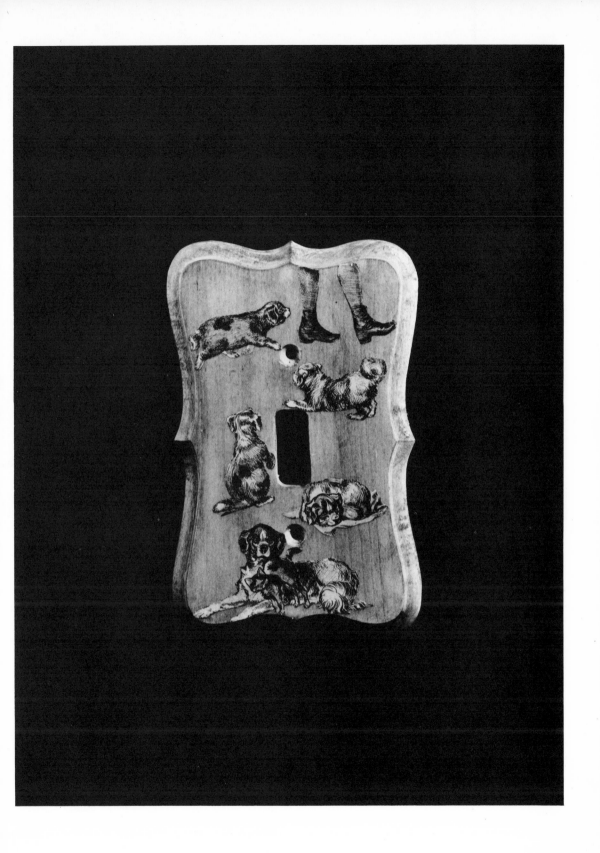

Figure 33. Another switchplate. This one was stained a natural mahogany. The feet at the top right again show how you can express a sense of humor with decoupage designs.

Figure 34. Here one small box tells a charming romantic tale. The side scrolls are colored in soft green, which is carried through in the costumes of the little couple on top.

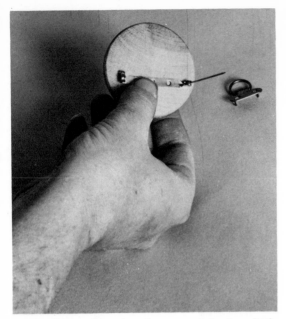

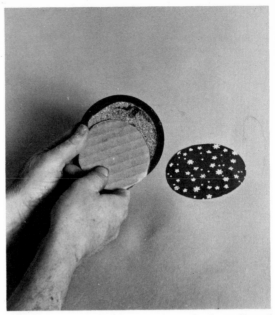

Decorating a Pin. Attach your pinback a little more than halfway down. If you also want your pin to hang, glue a pendant hook right above the pinback.

Decorating a Coaster. A corrugated cardboard circle has been cut to fit the hollowed part of a coaster. Here it is being glued in as a backing. An attractive piece of gift wrap will be pasted over the entire back.

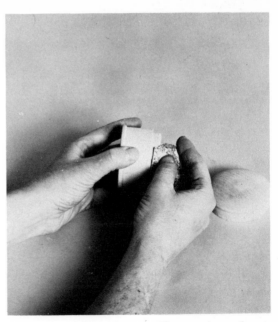

Decorating a Box. Step 1. Here is the type of box which would be a suitable size and shape for a starting project.

Decorating a Box. Step 2. The openings of your box must be carefully sanded to allow for the expansion of the wood during painting. Use regular sandpaper, torn into a small piece, and sand until the box fit is quite loose.

Decorating a Box. *Step 3. Here is the box being painted with a hand-mixed formula of gesso and acrylic paint from the tube. The formula in this case was two teaspoons of royal blue into the 4-oz. jar of gesso. The result was a lovely baby blue.*

Decorating a Box. *Step 4. Sometimes a design which seems appropriate looks all wrong when it is held against the box. Although this design is attractive, it would look grotesque because the lady's head would overlap the edge of the lid.*

Decorating a Box. *Step 5. A temporary sticking glue makes it possible to test a design. This time, everything seems to be working out.*

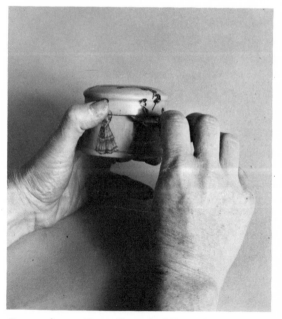

Decorating a Box. *Step 6. When the design has been glued down, a single-edged razor blade is used to cut the figures which cross the box opening.*

4

ROCK DECOUPAGE

Some of the most exciting decoupage possibilities may be found right in your own back yard or at a nearby park. If you love the shiny patina of a well-finished piece of wood or metal decoupage, just wait until you feel a rock or stone which has been well varnished or rubbed. Even people who have not yet been fired with enthusiasm for decoupage become inspired by rock decoupage.

As you varnish your stones, you will discover that designs sink faster into stone than other materials, probably because it is a less porous substance. A design which might take twenty-five coats of varnish to sink into wood, might be done in just twelve or fifteen coats on a stone.

Being a rock hound offers a lot of fun in itself. If you live near a beach, by all means take a walk along the shore soon. Any day is a good day, but the day after a storm is best since that is when the ocean will wash ashore the most interesting treasures. Take along a pail or a strong bag in which to gather your finds.

Rock Treasures and Shapes

The rocks should feel smooth in the hand when you find them. Unlike wood which can be sanded smooth if the surface is rough textured, a rock has a surface whose basic "feel" will not be altered by sanding. Indeed you would not want to alter the rock's texture since its whole appeal is that of a natural material. There are many beautifully shaped stones with pebbly, rough-grained surfaces. These are of interest to the general rock hound. The decoupage-minded rock hound is interested only in those stones which have an over-all smooth feel. The decoupage finish will emphasize and enrich this natural smoothness, but not create it.

But do not expect to find stones without *some* imperfections. A few little dents and crevices are perfectly all right as long as the major portion of the design plan is free of graininess and indentations. In fact, a dent or crevice here and there can be made to work for you in designing. A figure in a sitting position may gracefully perch on a crevice. By using this crevice as a seat it becomes an integral part of your design. A crack or crevice may also be utilized to suggest a cloud in an outdoor scene. (See the Demonstration on rocks at the end of the chapter.)

In order to help you search for and choose rocks, I will describe some of the things a decoupeur can do with rocks.

Paperweights

Large stones which lie down flat to show one design surface are ideal for paperweights. These come in many different shades and offer a generous and interesting design surface. While you will be decorating only the top surface, the edges show enough of a side to allow a bit of design to slope down across the edge if you so desire (Figure 36).

Small Sculptures

Some of the best stones stand up so that they can be designed on two or more surfaces (Figures 37 and 38). Usually these are fairly big stones, though at times a small stone has these stand-up qualities (Figure 39). Stones with this multilevel quality have a three-dimensional sculptured effect and can be displayed as sculptures in any home. They can, of course, also do double duty as paperweights.

Pictures on Easels

Some less interesting stones can be turned into fascinating easel pictures by using small backup

Figure 35. Here is a handsome table-top sculpture. The stone was dark gray, which looks magnificent under varnish and offers a fine background for the figures, which are rust, red, beige, soft green, blue, and pink. The figures are from The Pied Piper of Hamelin *and they dance all around the rock.*

Figure 36. This stone has the perfect shape for a paperweight. It came with a handsome two-tone shading of dark gray and white. The designs are colored in brilliant orange and green.

Figure 37. A large stone, which leans in a most interesting way, offered a real designing challenge. The natural beige color was enhanced and deepened with a touch of wood stain rubbed into the crevices. (See Color Plate 5.)

Figure 38. Another distinguished-looking rock had a natural shade of light gray. The scrolls which go all around the rock are done in a rich blue which is carried through in the peasant costumes. Greens and yellows are used as accent colors.

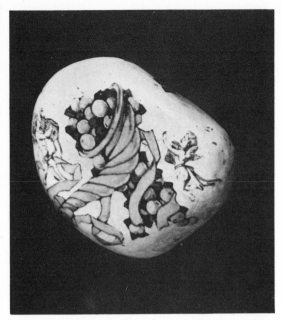

Figure 39. *Even small rocks sometimes stand up by themselves and offer all around designing surface. This rock was handsomely proportioned but a rather dull gray. It was lightened by washing in some white paint. The fruit baskets were colored in gold, with the fruits in shades of red. The little angel leads into another fruit basket not seen here.*

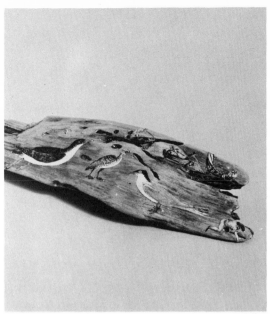

Figure 40. *One natural material leads to another. Since stones offered such exciting decoupage possibilities, driftwood seemed another "natural," especially when used as a background for a seascape. The uneven broken pieces of the driftwood edges served as water. The wood took to the varnish finish beautifully.*

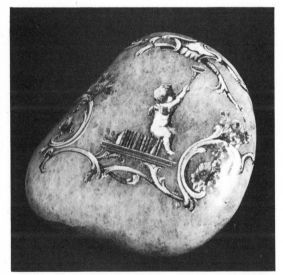

Figure 41. *A stone, which would have looked rather undistinguished lying down, is made to sit up by cementing on a backup stone. This gives a much better view of the design.*

Figure 42. *A rock ring is sure to be a conversation piece, and even though the surface is small, you can create a variety of designs. The finger ring was stained with gold paint and decorated with a clasped hand design for friendship. The center ring was wood stained and has two peace doves nesting atop a shocking pink scroll. The ring at right was painted black with a bow and head scroll left black and white.*

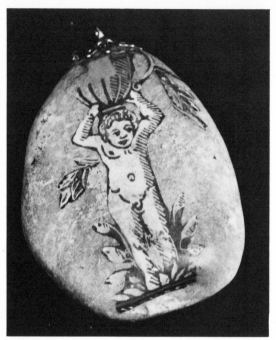

Figure 43. A stone pendant is another very special piece of jewelry, easy to design. This one is designed with a small zodiac sign. The back is also designed since pendants do swing freely and tend to turn.

Figure 44. Another dramatic pendant is done on a piece of slate. The irregularities add to the natural look and make for a more interesting design. The faces on the top right and left sides are on a lower level than the center designs. The slate is very dark gray, almost black. The faces are in brilliant flesh tones, with green eyes and facial shadows and touches of red and yellow.(See Color Plate 11.)

stones as an easel (Figure 41). These would be flat stones which have good smooth surfaces, but are too thin and lightweight to serve as effective paperweights. By using a small stone with one flat surface as you would an easel, these flat unimportant-looking stones stand up so that any decoupage design can be put into proper focus. The backup stones can be completely rough and craggy since they will be used like hardware rather than as design surfaces. They must have one flat surface which will fit the back of the main stone. Quite often a broken stone will serve this purpose. The backup stone must be cemented on with a strong cement such as epoxy. (See the Demonstration on rocks at the end of the chapter.)

Rings

If you love chunky rings, keep your eyes open for smooth, oblong, or abstract shapes. A rock with a length of approximately ¾" will give you sufficient space to make an appealing ring design and will not be too bulky even on a small hand. Tiny clasped hands to express friendship or initials, flowers, zodiac symbols are just a few of the types of cutouts which work well into a ring design (Figure 42).

To make the ring wearable you will need a base with a slightly concave surface to which the stone can be cemented. These are very inexpensive and have adjustable bands (see Jewelry Suppliers List). (See the Demonstration on rocks at the end of the chapter.)

Pendants

A jewelry finding known as a bellcap can be cemented to a stone so that it can be hung from a chain and worn as an eye-catching pendant. Stones for this purpose should be lightweight and no thicker than ½". They can be designed on two sides. (See Figure 43 and the Demonstration on rocks at the end of the chapter.)

Another stone material which can be used for this purpose is slate. You do not have to be put off by uneven edges. These give wonderful free-form effects to what you do. However, be sure that your piece of slate is solid enough not to crumble. Take the slate firmly in hand and bend it as if to break it. Some types of slate will crumble when you apply this sort of pressure to them (See the example in Figure 44).

Sources for Rocks

The small and medium-size rocks will be easy to find, be it at the seashore or in a park. You might have to search a bit for any really big rocks. If your trips to the shore or local park are unsuccessful, look in your telephone directory for a stone or mason supply company. There is one in every town, no matter how small, and they will let you go through their pile and pick out two or three. Chances are excellent that they will shrug away your offers to pay.

Preparing a Rock for Finishing

To prepare your rock, first scrub it with soap and water, and dry.

Study your rock from all angles. See which way it "sits." If it narrows to a point, turn it with the point at different angles to determine which way to plan your design. If it rests securely on several surfaces, try it out each way and decide which surface makes you think of the best design possibilities. Study the crevices and cracks to see if they can be worked into your picture or if it would be best to turn them towards the bottom. (See the Demonstration on decorating a rock, *Step 1*, at the end of the chapter.)

Consider the stone's coloring and the colors you plan for your picture. Most stones have lovely natural colors: dark and light grays and mixtures thereof, and almost clear whites and beiges. Generally, stones are beautiful when their natural colors are left intact. The varnish finish will bring out the natural tones.

Coloring

Sometimes you will find a stone you love of which the natural color is not to your taste or not in keeping with a planned design. These stones can be painted any color you wish, with either water- or oil-based paints. No sealing is necessary to prepare the stone for paint. One coat of paint is usually sufficient to cover.

When I make any color alterations, I prefer to let at least some of the natural color show through. Thus, instead of brushing on a solid coat of paint, I wash in my paint like a glaze. For example, if I want to lighten a pale gray stone, I take a damp rag or a piece of foam and dip it lightly into some white paint. I rub this in very gently. If I have put on too much paint, I quickly dampen a rag with water and remove some but not all of my paint. The result will be more natural: a bleached, almost white gray, rather than a painted stone. (See the Demonstration on decorating a rock, *Step 3*, at the end of the chapter.)

For a tan stone, I like to dip a rag into a liquid brown wood stain (or you could use a rag dipped into turpentine with a dab of Turkey Umber from a tube of artist's oils). I rub this into my stone like furniture polish. After a few minutes I wipe the stone clean with a lintless rag, allowing the stain to remain embedded in any crevice. You can use colors other than white, or stains other than wood tones to give your stone this kind of color glaze.

Any attachments such as backup stones to make the rock stand up, or jewelry findings for pendants, should be attached before you start designing or varnishing.

Finishing the Design

Glue your design. This must be done with special care since you are likely to be working with a less than perfectly smooth ground. Take extra care to press out bumps and to fit your paper into and around crevices which might become air bubble traps. (See the Demonstration on decorating a rock, *Step 5*, at the end of the chapter.)

Apply your finish. About fifteen coats of varnish should completely sink in your designs. Small items such as pendants and rings might be complete sooner.

To finish off backs and bottoms of stones, two coats of finish applied to the "hidden" parts will give the over-all stone a feeling of uniformity. These lightly varnished backs need not be sanded. Rub them very lightly with steel wool, and wax along with the entire stone. Glue a piece of felt to the bottom of a very heavy rock to prevent it from scratching table and shelf tops.

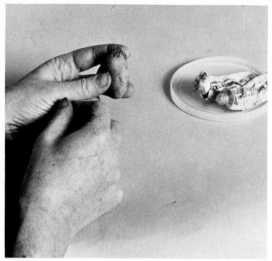

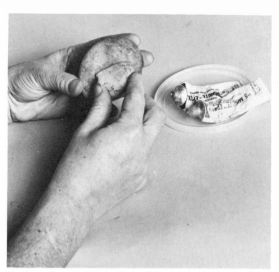

Drying. Bellcaps. A jewelry finding known as a bellcap has all around prongs which can be opened up and adjusted to fit around a stone to be used as a pendant. The finding should be attached with epoxy.

Drying. Easel effect. A small stone with a flat back is cemented with a strong epoxy to a larger flat stone to achieve a stand-up easel effect.

Drying. Attaching a base. Cement your stone to the ring base before you start designing.

Rocks. The crevices in this rock look like clouds hovering over the dancing figures.

Decorating a Rock. Step 1. *Inspect your rock from all angles. This rock offers many possibilities.*

Decorating a Rock. Step 2. *The irregular crack going across the rock at this angle provided an interesting ledge for a design of seated figures.*

Decorating a Rock. Step 3. *A sponge dipped lightly into diluted white paint is gently rubbed against the stone to whitewash the natural gray color.*

Decorating a Rock. Step 4. *The design is tacked down. The crevice worked out fine as a ledge for the angel figures.*

Decorating a Rock. Step 5. *A spoon is used to smooth the figures into that crevice, to make sure no air bubbles are left when the gluing is complete.*

5

PAPIER-MACHE DECOUPAGE

One of the most interesting aspects of decoupage is working with new shapes and materials. It is great fun to browse through antique and junk shops in search of unusually shaped items. There is a real thrill in ferreting through other people's discards and coming upon a perfect decoupage base. Among my best finds were a builder friend's old cabinet door samples heaped right on top of his garbage. These are now among my most attractive plaques (Figures 48 and 49).

When I was at a crafts exhibition one year, many visitors picked up my work and asked, "Did you make this?" referring to the background as well as the surface design. Their questions presented a new challenge. A true craftsman *should* be able to travel the whole route by making something from scratch! Since decoupage is a paper art, papier-mâché seemed the first and most likely method for achieving a "total" product. This combination of mâché and decoupage proved a very happy marriage of two fine old crafts.

It is the layering of paper and the slow-drying process that makes papier-mâché very sturdy. Papier-mâché furniture and decorative objects made a hundred years ago are still in use and greatly treasured. The decoupage finishing process of varnishing and rubbing will add still more durability and beauty.

Materials for Papier-Mâché

The materials for the papier-mâché are mostly around-the-house supplies. Here's what you will need.

Cardboards. Lightweight cardboards such as the type used by laundries to pack shirts, and corrugated cardboard of the weight and thickness found in grocery cartons.

Newspapers. This is the actual paper in papier-mâché.

Strong scissors. To cut through light cardboard and layers of newspaper.

White glue. Diluted by one third with water, or, if you plan to make quite a lot of things in papier-mâché and want an equally effective and more economical paste, use wheat paste. This is the wallpaper hangers' paste and is available in all paint supply stores with directions for mixing and applying.

Instant papier-mâché. This is ground-up paper pulp sold by the pound in every art supply store. The gray pulp is mixed with water to form a mash which feels and works like clay. It dries rock hard, can be sanded and painted, and is very effective for a variety of purposes. In this chapter it will be used for making a pin with a raised, rounded surface and for repair work. In Chapter 12, you will learn additional uses to which instant papier-mâché can be put.

Acrylic gesso. This is important for coating your dried and finished mâché items; it acts as a sealer and prevents warping.

Papier-Mâché Techniques

Since we aim for a smooth surface in decoupage, I will give you directions for building up newspapers into evenly cut and measured layers. Papier-mâché "purists" usually prefer to work with torn paper strips applied in a more casual and crisscross manner. For those of you who wish to explore papier-mâché in depth there are a number of excellent books available on the subject which you will find listed in the Bibliography.

Making a Plaque

The plaque shown in the step-by-step demonstration at the end of the chapter has a three-dimensional raised look. To achieve this you will actually be making two plaques, one somewhat larger than the other. The illustrated model is an oval shape, but it could have been round, square, rectangular, or any other shape.

Cutting

To begin, cut two ovals out of corrugated cardboard. One oval will be ½" smaller than the other. (See the Demonstration on making a plaque, *Step 1*, at the end of the chapter.) You can trace the diagram for the illustrated plaque for your first effort (Figure 45). Art supply stores sell plastic templates with the graduated sizes of ovals, ellipses, and other shapes. These can be used as guides for making your plaque outlines. Or, you can make a perfectly proportioned oval by interconnecting three circles (Figure 46).

Cut twenty-one newspaper squares. Ten inches by ten inches would be right for the sample ovals. Lay aside the twenty-first square and draw the outline of the oval on this oval.

Outline the larger cardboard oval twice on the top square. (See the Demonstration on making a plaque, *Step 2*, at the end of the chapter).

Glue your newspaper squares one on top of the other, sandwich fashion. Be sure to smooth out wrinkles before applying each new layer. (See the Demonstration on decorating a plaque, *Step 3*, at the end of the chapter.)

Your newspaper squares are now all glued together (except for the extra square). The squares with the outlined ovals are on top. Cut out each of these ovals. (See the Demonstration on making a plaque, *Step 4*, at the end of the chapter.)

Glue one of these newspaper ovals to each side of the larger corrugated oval. (See the Demonstration on making a plaque, *Step 5*, at the end of the chapter.)

Now repeat these steps for the smaller oval. Cut out twenty-one more newspaper squares—laying one aside with the small oval outlined on the spare one, as before. Outline the smaller oval twice on the top newspaper square. Glue all your newspaper squares together. Cut around the oval outlines of the glued-together squares. Glue one glued-together newspaper oval to each side of the smaller corrugated oval.

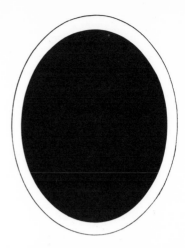

Figure 45. Here is an oval which, with a little practice, you will find easy to draw. Try tracing this one until you get the feel of how to draw it.

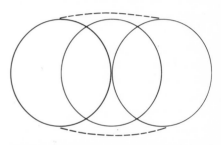

Figure 46. This diagram shows how you can make your own oval with 3 circles. First draw the center circle using a compass. Now place your second circle so that one of its edges touches the center point of the first circle and draw another circle extending out to the right of the first circle. Using the same method, draw a third circle to the left. Make the circles into an oval (see dotted lines).

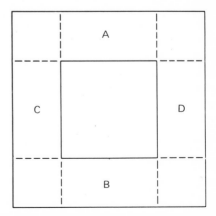

Figure 47. This is the base for a box. Cut through the broken lines to get corners which will fit smoothly together. Next bend sides A, B, C, D upward along the solid lines and tape the sides.

When you have assembled the smaller oval, center it against the larger and glue together. (See the Demonstration on making a plaque, *Step 6*, at the end of the chapter.)

Finishing the Form

Tear off small newspaper strips, approximately 1" by ½", dip these into glue, and smooth them from the edge of the smaller oval over and across the outside edge of the larger oval. Apply these strips until all the edges of the corrugated cardboard are covered with newspaper. (See the Demonstration on making a plaque, *Step 7*, at the end of the chapter.)

Now take those set aside newspaper squares, cut out the oval, and attach one over the front of the plaque, and the larger over the back of the plaque. These will hide the uneven edges of those small pasted strips. (See the Demonstration on making a plaque, *Step 8*, at the end of the chapter.)

Drying

Your plaque is ready to dry. Put a piece of wax paper between the damp newspaper and the weight (a heavy book or rock) to protect the layered surface against any rips. This weighting is very important since the layered newspaper and glue tend to contract during drying and unless your plaque is properly weighted it will warp. (See the Demonstration on making a plaque, *Step 9*, at the end of the chapter.) You can dry the plaque naturally; in the summertime, the sunshine is ideal, and a boiler room offers very controlled heat. A very slow oven, 170 degrees, with the door open, for about a half hour, would also be suitable.

When your plaque is dry, apply two thin coats of gesso to both front and back. Your gesso can serve as a background, or you can paint over the gesso. You can sand lightly between the applications, for extra smoothness. (See the Demonstration on making a plaque, *Step 10*, at the end of the chapter.)

Finishing the Plaque

First, design your plaque. You could extend your design across the rim of the plaque, or simply emphasize any unevenness left by the little connecting strips with a touch of gold rubbed on the rim. (See the Demonstration on making a plaque, *Steps 11 and 12*, at the end of this chapter.)

Making a Pin-Pendant

Making a pin-pendant involves the same procedure as the plaque, except that you are working with a single layer. These pin-pendants can also be used as key chains, mini-plaques, and since papier-mâché is so light, they would make very comfortable earrings. The shape variations are practically limitless and once you become adept at layering the newspaper squares you can set up your own "mass production" system by cutting several shapes out of one set of newspaper layers. (See the Demonstration on making a pin-pendant at the end of the chapter.)

Let's just go through the steps for a pin-pendant giving dimensions for a circle.

Cutting

Cut a 2¾' circle out of corrugated cardboard. Then, cut twenty 6" squares out of newspaper and separate into two stacks of ten each.

Outline your cardboard circle twice on the newspaper square which will be your top layer and glue your newspaper squares together. Then, cut out the two outlined circles and paste one on each side of the corrugated cardboard. Finally, cut a strip of lightweight cardboard to go around the corrugated edge. This will help keep the shape as well as hide the open edges.

If you plan to wear this as a pendant, it is now ready to be weighted for drying. (See the Demonstration on making a pin-pendant at the end of the chapter.)

Alternative Surfaces

If you want a pin or pendant with a raised, curved look, mix a small amount of instant papier-mâché with water. (Any unused portions of this material can be stored indefinitely in a plastic bag or container in the refrigerator. Press a patty approximately the size of your pin between the palms of your hands. Put glue on top of your pin and press the patty down, shaping it as you go along, so that the mash thins down along the edges. (See the Demonstration on making a pin-pendant at the end of the chapter.)

Since this type of pin is not flat it cannot be weighted down with anything that would ruin the shape of the mash top. However, you *could* use an ovenproof glass about ½" smaller than the pin to weight the edges.

Drying

Dry your pendant slowly. When it is dry, you could drill a hole for a chain, earring loops, or a key ring. The dried pin can be sanded smooth with a rough grade of sandpaper. For extra smoothness before painting and designing, you could paste down a circle of newspaper on top of the mash, molding this carefully to avoid wrinkles.

Making a Box

We will be using lightweight cardboard for the base of the box, and corrugated cardboard for the lid. The sample is 3" square. This size can of course be adjusted to your own needs.

To make a box, first draw a 6" square on lightweight cardboard and section off 1½" all around for the box sides.

Fold up the sides and cut off the corners (Figure 47). Then, tape your sides together with masking tape. (See the Demonstration on making a box, *Step 1*, at the end of the chapter.)

Cutting

Cut twelve strips of newspaper 3" by 12". Paste six strips together, making sure to smooth out all wrinkles. Then, take this glued-together layer of newspaper strips and glue from inside and all around the other side of the box, so that the end of your newspaper strip meets the beginning. (See the Demonstration on making a box, *Step 2*, at the end of the chapter.)

Take your leftover six strips of newspaper and glue them together. Then, take the second set of glued-together newspapers and bring them around the other side of the box. Your sides are now reinforced with six layers of newspapers, and the bottom of the box with twice as many. (See the Demonstration on making a box, *Step 3*, at the end of the chapter.)

The Box Top

The box top is made just like the papier-mâché plaque, with two pieces of corrugated cardboard, one smaller than the other, and each one layered on both sides with glued-together newspapers.

First, cut a pattern out of corrugated cardboard for the lid. This should be 3" square if you want the top the exact same size as the box; 3½" square

if you like an overlapping look. (See Figures 4 and 53).

Now, make a corrugated pattern for the inner rim. A 2¼" square will allow the lid to fit comfortably inside the box. Cut twenty-one newspaper squares (about 5" or 6" square). Set one square aside. Next, outline the larger cardboard square twice on the newspaper which will be your top layer, and once on the set-aside square. Glue your newspaper squares together. Cut out the two outlined squares and paste one to each side of the box lid. Repeat these steps for the box rim (inside lid).

The next step is to center the rim against the box lid and glue together. Make sure your lid fits properly before you go any further. Take small strips of newspaper and paste these from the rim over across the outside of the lid, until all the corrugated edges are covered with newspaper strips. Now, take your extra square from the lid and your extra square from the rim and paste on. For a softer look, take a strong scissors and round off the corners of your lid. (See the Demonstration on making a box, *Step 4*, at the end of the chapter.)

To insure that the box keeps its shape during drying, stuff with crumpled wax paper. Put on the lid. Cover the whole thing with a protective layer of wax paper and tape up with masking tape or tie with string.

Papier-Mâché to Make Repairs

In addition to using papier-mâché to build your own base, you can apply this knowledge to repairing damaged items which you would like to decoupage. A finish which might take immeasurable hours of elbow grease to strip and repaint, can be revitalized and strengthened with layers of newspaper strips dipped into paste. When this finish is painted with two layers of gesso on each side, sanded smooth, and ready to decoupage, you will have something really special. Deep cracks can be filled in with instant papier-mâché. (See the Demonstration on papier-mâché repair at the end of the chapter and Figure 55.)

Old papier-mâché items in good condition are very costly to obtain. However, once you know how to work with papier-mâché, you might concentrate some of your treasure hunts through flea markets and antique shops on trying to find papier-mâché trays and other items which are nicked and damaged. Because of their condition, the price is likely to be more than reasonable.

Figure 48. One man's discard becomes a decoupeur's treasure. To wit, this lovely plaque designed on a base that was once a kitchen cabinet sample. The Godey ladies are hand colored. The curtains and door which overlap the rim suggest a whole room.

Figure 49. Another sample for a kitchen cabinet. This time a yellow ground with shades of pink and gray highlighting the designs. The decorations on the mantel, the wall sconces, and the mirror were from diverse sources. The fireplace was from a stage print.

Figure 50. *A papier-mâché plaque. The edges are rubbed with gold, which gives an antique wood look to the plaque. The figures and fruit and flower border are colored in blues and greens, which gives a harmonious feeling.*

Figure 51. A papier-mâché pendant bears a message of "love."

Figure 52. The shapes which papier-mâché pendants and pins can take are limitless. Here's a hexagon, painted black on one side, white on the other. The design we see is a circle of hands, surrounded by daisies. The second side has a musical theme of little dancing figures on a border of musical notes.

Figure 53. Here is a papier-mâché box of handsome proportions. The design is predominantly yellow against black.

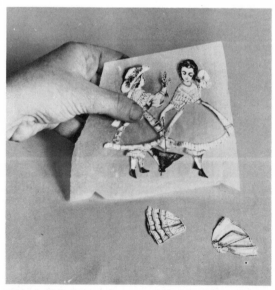

Figure 54. To make a multilevel picture from a pre-existing print, first study the print to see which portions can be raised. The skirts of these two little girls can be raised up and molded.

Figure 55. *This frame was a wreck, full of nicks, and covered with layers and layers of old paint. Papier-mâché strips were used to repair it, and it is now a handsome mirror designed with a lovely alphabet by Kate Greenaway.*

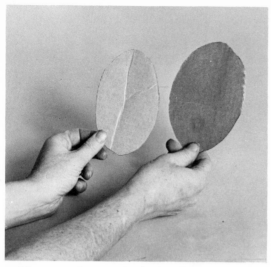

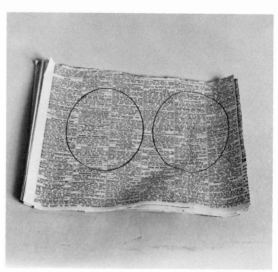

Making a Plaque. Step 1. Two corrugated cardboard ovals serve as the base for the plaques. Corrugated cardboard is used since it is less subject to warpage.

Making a Plaque. Step 2. Stacks of newspaper squares will be layered together. The outline of the plaque is drawn on the layer to end up on top.

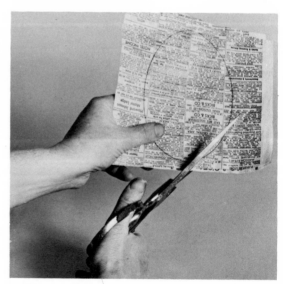

Making a Plaque. Step 3. The squares are glued together, with the wrinkles carefully pressed out before a new square is attached.

Making a Plaque. Step 4. When the squares are glued and smoothed together, the oval outlines are cut out.

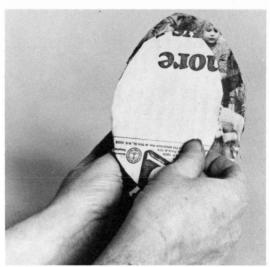

Making a Plaque. Step 5. An oval of glued-together newspaper is glued to each side of the corrugated oval and pressed down tightly.

Making a Plaque. Step 6. The smaller oval, also covered on each side with layered, glued-together newspapers, is centered against the larger one and glued on.

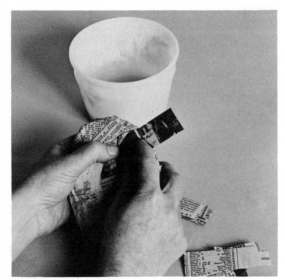

Making a Plaque. Step 7. Small strips of newspaper are dipped in glue and used to connect the smaller and larger oval, giving a smooth edge.

Making a Plaque. Step 8. The laid-aside newspaper ovals are now pasted onto each side of the plaque to hide the marks of newspaper strip edges.

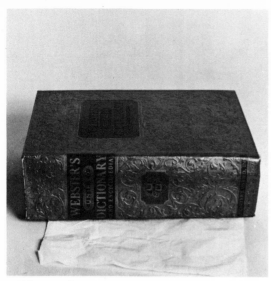

Making a Plaque. Step 9. The plaque is covered with protective wax paper and weighted down under a heavy book to prevent warpage during drying.

Making a Plaque. Step 10. When the plaque is dry, it is painted twice on each side with gesso.

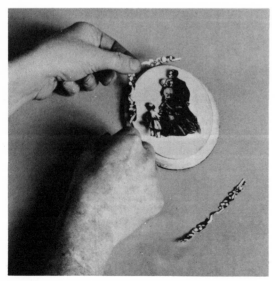

Making a Plaque. Step 11. The decoupage design is planned.

Making a Plaque. Step 12. A touch of gold wax is rubbed around the rim of the plaque.

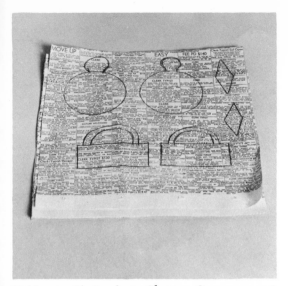

Making a Pin-Pendant. Shapes. *Once you get accustomed to layering the newspapers, you can make several pins, pendants, and key chains at once. Here is a sample square with just some of the possibilities for shapes which would lend themselves to good designs.*

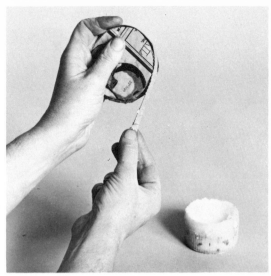

Making a Pin-Pendant. Edges. *A strip of lightweight cardboard hides the corrugated edges of the pendant and helps keep the shape.*

Making a Pin-Pendant. Surfaces. *A patty of instant papier-mâché is glued to the pendant to give a raised, curved look.*

Making a Box. Step 1. *The bottom of the box is cut out and the corners taped up.*

Making a Box. Step 2. *Newspaper strips being adhered across the sides, outside, other side, and back around the inside bottom of the box.*

Making a Box. Step 3. *The newspaper layers being adhered the other way, so that six layers of newspaper cover each side, and the bottom has been reinforced each time, comprising a total of twelve layers.*

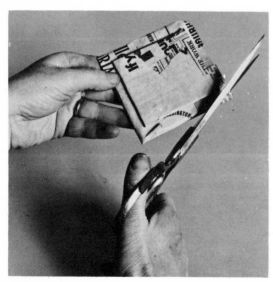

Making a Box. Step 4. *Here is the box lid with the corners of the rim rounded off for a better look. The box should now be completely taped up for warpage-free drying.*

Papier-Mâché Repair. *Here is an example of repairing an otherwise hopelessly damaged frame with pieces of papier-mâché dipped in paste.*

6

DECOUPAGE AND THE THIRD DIMENSION

When you use your coloring pencils to emphasize the curve of a flower and when you cut your print with a zigzag rather than a straight edge, you are automatically adding dimension to your finished picture. You can actually raise portions of your design to achieve a true third dimension. Some three-dimensional techniques are quite simple and require little or no finish coating, and no rubbing at all. Others are somewhat more complicated. Here are some of the ways of achieving the third dimension.

The Multilevel Picture

This is usually done inside a deep frame. Using your cutting and coloring skills and your imagination as a designer, you create a scene in which portions are flat and others are raised up by means of bits of cork or cardboard. In this way, a figure actually casts a realistic shadow; hence the expression, shadow box.

Depending upon the size and dimension of your scene you can have just two levels, the flat background and raised-up figures in the forefront. You could raise some of the figures with more cardboard than others, thus achieving a three-level effect.

The multilevel picture you create by taking bits and pieces of scenery and figures to create a scene of your own invention is the most fun to do (Figure 60). At its simplest, the multilevel picture takes an already existing scene and gives it a new look by introducing different levels of depth.

Making a Multilevel Picture

An illustration from a children's book is carefully studied to see where portions could be raised to give an added dimension. The material in the background is always raised up less than the foreground material. Thus, the rear wall stayed in place, but two buildings were cut apart to create a passageway. The raised portion was created by one level of fairly thick cardboard.

The portion of the picture at the front—the lawn and the large figure of the boy—was raised up with two levels of cardboard. (See the Demonstration on making a multilevel picture, *Step 1*, at the end of the chapter.)

In order to take advantage of the three-dimensional effect created by this cutting apart of the picture, a few additions were made. A small figure of a mother holding a baby and a running child were placed in the little passageway between the buildings in the rear. A young lady was placed near the gate, as if she were going to meet the boy in the foreground. These little figures were taken from other portions of the book from which this illustration was taken and were thus in keeping with the over-all scene.

While the shadows cast by the raised-up sections of the picture would hide any holes left in the background sections, a few adjustments were made so that the picture would look complete even if someone looked at it from the side. To do this, little windows with little heads peeking out were put into the house out of which the little lady at the gate came.

The finished picture was coated with about three coats of varnish and placed inside a deep frame. (See the Demonstration on making a multilevel picture, *Step 2*, at the end of the chapter.)

Suitable Materials

In choosing pictures for three-dimensional use it is not necessary to look for papers thin enough to sink into varnish. In fact, paper with some body is

Figure 56. *This picture combines two three-dimensional techniques. First, an original raised level picture was created. The fiddler, dog, and poster were pasted against a brick wall of pink poster board, with the bricks penciled in. Two little-girl prints were hand colored, cut, and raised against cardboard to create a shadow-box effect. To give further dimension to this scene, another print was used to cut out portions of the children's skirts and sleeves. (See Color Plate 9.)*

Figure 57. *A sculptured paper on Papier Tole picture created from two copies of a Dufy print. Even the vase which holds the flowers has been sculptured up. The flower at top hangs over the matting. The more you cut into the flowers and the more you raise, the more attractive these pictures are.*

Figure 58. *Gift-wrap papers seem made for the paper sculpturing since they usually are packed with double sheets. The gift wrap here was rearranged to achieve a new composition.*

Figure 59. *The skirts of the girls' dresses were stuffed with bread dough. When this hardened, the stuffed print was pasted to the rest and everything was varnished together, sanded, and rubbed. In paper sculpture, the edges are left loose.*

preferable. If you use lightweight paper (the average black and white decoupage print or regular typing paper) you can easily give it body by pasting it against another piece of plain paper.

As for finishing, you can simply enclose your picture behind a protective glass. I prefer to coat mine with three or four coats of varnish which (since it will not be rubbed down) will have a nice sheen. The protective varnish will make your paper stiff and durable. A varnished picture will be protected from dirt, and has an added feeling of dimension because you can actually reach out and touch its surface.

Sculptured Paper Pictures

One of the fastest and most modern ways to achieve a three-dimensional look for your decoupage is to use two identical prints and a few dabs of clear silicone caulking from the hardware store. This silicone glue serves to hold and raise the prints. Patricia Nimocks was the first to popularize this modern offshoot of stuffed and molded decoupage, and she gave it the elegant name of Papier Tole.

In doing this type of paper sculpture, one print serves as a background print while portions of the second are cut up so that they can be contoured and raised over the matching background. The edges are left loose and a dab of silicone stands between background and top portions. Silicone is a wonderful modern material. It hardens and holds the top print firmly and lastingly (Figure 57).

Flowers are the most popular subjects for these sculptured pictures, though figures with billowing skirts and sleeves work out very well too. You can use either hand-colored or ready-colored prints, but whatever you choose, your paper must have body so that it will lend itself to contouring. There are many attractive and inexpensive pictures available which are too light to use "as is" but which can be given just the right amount of body if you back them with another piece of paper.

Gift wraps are a rich source for paper sculptures and seem *made* for this type of decoupage since they come packaged in large duplicate sheets. They need to be stiffened with backing paper.

Making a Gift-Wrap Paper Sculpture

The gift-wrap flowers and butterfly picture made in the step-by-step demonstration involved quite a lot of rearranging of the print materials, elimina-

Figure 60. Bookends with scenes from old school primers are arranged in a mosaic layout. The upper bookend uses borders made up of counting illustrations from an arithmetic primer. The bookend right above is bordered with headings from the book, showing how effectively type can be used in design. The prints were left uncolored against a canary yellow background. This is a stunning color combination. (See Color Plate 17.)

ting the ribbons, and placing all the flowers in a hand-drawn vase. This adds an extra dimension in creativity. Many prints can simply be used as background, with portions to be raised cut out of a second print and placed over the matching parts for a composite scene. Here is how to make giftwrap flower pictures.

The portions to be used for the bouquet were cut out in duplicate. Then, a sheet of plain paper was pasted to the flowers to be raised up to give extra body. The background flowers did not need to be reinforced with extra paper. (See the Demonstration on making a paper sculpture, *Step 1*, at the end of the chapter.)

A simple flower base was cut out and colored and pasted to the plaque backing. Then, the background (in other words, the flat portion of the design) was pasted into place. The parts to be raised were carefully cut and molded and contoured in the palm of the hand. The easiest way to give this molded contour to your print is to lay it face down in the palm of your hand and then run your thumb from the center out to the edge until the flower curls up. (See the Demonstration on making a paper sculpture, *Step 2*, at the end of the chapter.)

Sometimes, of course, you may want a leaf to flip up rather than down and then you would reverse this procedure. The more you cut into the leaves and buds and flowers to be raised, the more lifelike and interesting your contouring effects will be.

Now, put a glob of the clear glue into the center of the print to be raised. I like to apply this with a toothpick. You could put the glue onto the background and then sit the raised, contoured print on top of that. It is up to you. Just be sure that your glob of glue is thick enough to give the print enough of a raised look. (See the Demonstration on making a paper sculpture, *Step 3*, at the end of the chapter.)

Do not press down on the print the way you do when you glue something down with white glue. The print and the glue underneath will feel loose and wiggly for at least ten minutes. Then the glue will harden and the top will adhere firmly. Any glue which oozes out in the wrong spot can be cleaned off with a toothpick.

Your sculptured picture can be put on a wooden plaque without a frame. It will look especially nice in a deep frame. There is no rubbing. The picture can be framed under glass, or coated with varnish.

Combining Three-Dimensional Techniques

Many prints lend themselves to treatment in any one of or a combination of three-dimensional techniques. An attractive print of two little girls with billowing skirts and sleeves would lend itself to being combined into an interesting scene with the girls on a raised level with silicone paper sculpturing for their skirts and sleeves. The picture combining the two techniques used a background of pink oak tag with a hand-drawn brick wall, and a group of figures from a book. The little girls completed the scene. They were first raised against cardboard. Then a second print was used to cut out portions of the costume which were then molded and sculptured and attached with silicone. These same little girls were used again for another type of three-dimensional decoupage: a method of stuffing and molding portions of a print known as "repoussé."

Stuffed and Molded Pictures—Repoussé

The sculptured or papier tole technique is actually a modern simplification of a much more complicated process known by its French name, repoussé, which means "to raise up." Instead of the raised portions of a print remaining loose at the edges, they are actually stuffed. Then, when dry and hard, these raised prints are glued to the flat part of the design.

Stuffed and molded designs can be protected under glass, or varnished and rubbed in the fine decoupage manner.

The best and easiest stuffing for these molded prints is bread dough.

Bread Dough Recipe

Take one slice of white bread. Remove the crusts and crumble up into a bowl. Add to this a scant teaspoon of white glue and a few drops of glycerine.

Knead this mixture. It will be sticky at first. Keep kneading until it no longer sticks but forms a ball. To stuff the prints for our molded picture demonstration you will need just a small ball of this mixture pressed into a ¼" thick patty. You can keep your dough indefinitely in a sealed plastic bag or a container stored in the refrigerator. It might become a bit hard, but kneading at room temperature will work it up to the proper consistency again. Possibly, you will have to add glue.

Making a Stuffed and Molded Picture

In this demonstration we will be using the same little girls seen in the paper sculpture multilevel picture. You will again be using two prints.

Paste down the background picture. Then, cut out the portions to be stuffed and molded from the extra print. (See the Demonstration on repoussé, *Step 1*, at the end of the chapter.) If this is a lightweight print, it should be made stronger by gluing it against an extra sheet of paper.

Break off a piece of bread dough and form a patty about ¼" thick and not quite as big as the print to be stuffed. (See the Demonstration on repoussé, *Step 2*, at the end of the chapter.) Now, turn the print to be stuffed over, with the blank side facing you, and glue in the bread dough patty. (See the Demonstration on repoussé, *Step 3*, at the end of the chapter.)

Next, turn the whole thing around again and place it on a piece of wax paper and mold the print around the patty. Some people like to wet the print before stuffing it, but I prefer to save the wetting of the print for this part of the operation. I take a damp sponge and dampen the top of my print. Then, I use my fingers and sometimes the edge of a plastic spoon to contour and shape the print around the patty. The bread dough is soft and pliable so that you can push back little bits of dough that might ooze out at the edges, and also indent a line here and there to go with the shape and shading of the print. In this way you make the "bump" look more natural when it is completely dry and hard. (See the Demonstration on repoussé, *Step 4*, at the end of the chapter.)

When you are satisfied with the way the print is molded over the dough, put it on a cooky sheet, print side up, and let it dry in a very slow oven (170 degrees) for a half hour. Let the patty dry, out of the oven, overnight. At the end of that time the bread dough will be hard and firm.

Glue the hardened, stuffed, raised print into place. (See the Demonstration on repoussé, *Step 5*, at the end of the chapter.) The entire picture should now be varnished until all the design edges are sunk in. After the usual twenty or more coats of varnish, the design is sanded and rubbed.

Stuffing and Molding With a Single Print

The easiest way to stuff and mold is to use two prints but you can achieve the same results with some extra work. Here is what you would have to add to the procedure I have just described.

First, cut out the portion to be stuffed from the one and only print you will use. (See the Demonstration on stuffing a single print at the end of the chapter.)

Next, turn the print face down and temporarily attach a piece of tracing paper over the back of the hole. Then, turn your print face up again and color about ¼" of the inside section of this tracing paper filling, using a color just a little darker than the color used in the rest of the print. The purpose of this is to fill in the space which will be created by the raising of the stuffed portion. The darker coloring will have the look of shading.

Remove the tracing paper and cut out the fill-ins, leaving a ¼" to ½" border around the colored area.

Finally, glue the cut filled-in section into place. You may now mold the cut-out portions around the bread dough as before and glue onto the tracing paper background.

Flowers

If you decide to try stuffed and molded decoupage, why not make some extra bread dough and learn to use it in a way that can serve as a most attractive auxiliary? Bread dough flowers and little animals make handsome and sturdy trims for boxes, frames, and stands.

Making a Bread Dough Daisy

Cut a piece of floral wire about 4" long. You can use the kind that is already covered or the very lightweight wires bent in half and twisted together for extra strength. (You could also use a piece of ordinary wire and cover with floral tape.)

Make a small ball of dough the size of a pea. Then, dip your wire into white glue and slip your ball of dough around this. This will be the center of the daisy. (See the Demonstration on making a bread dough daisy, *Step 1*, at the end of the chapter.)

Now take another piece of bread dough and shape a piece about ½" by ¾". Use a cuticle scissors and make four slits for your petals. (See the Demonstration on making a bread dough daisy, *Step 2*, at the end of the chapter.)

Use your fingers to shape and thin the petals. (See the Demonstration on making a bread dough daisy, *Step 3*, at the end of the chapter.)

Put a dab of glue at the base of the petals, the part that is uncut, and attach this around the center of the daisy. Half your daisy will now be complete. Make another flat piece and glue this to complete the daisy. (See the Demonstration on making a bread dough daisy, *Step 4*, at the end of the chapter.) The daisy is ready for a finish.

Brush the flower with glue, diluted with water 50/50. You can brush this on with your fingers, a cotton swab, or a small brush. This will give your daisy a nice sheen when hard and also prevent breakage and shrinkage.

Figure 61. *The little girls in this print can be used to achieve three-dimensional effects either in the multilevel paper sculpture or repoussé technique. Raised portions should be backed with an extra sheet of paper for body.*

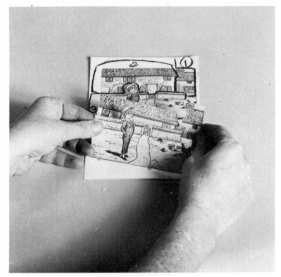

Making a Multilevel Picture. *Step 1. The scene to be made into a three-dimensional, multilevel picture is marked up. Section one will be raised up with one piece of carboard; section two, with two pieces of cardboard; section three, with three pieces of cardboard. Next to the marked-up scene you can see the cut-apart sections held up.*

Making a Multilevel Picture. *Step 2. Here is the finished multilevel picture inside a deep frame.*

Making a Paper Sculpture. *Step 1. The design was taken from two pieces of gift wrap. The sections which will be used for the paper-sculpture picture are backed up with an extra sheet of paper.*

Making a Paper Sculpture. *Step 2. The sections to be raised are contoured in the palm of the hand and shaped with the fingertips.*

Making a Paper Sculpture. Step 3. The contoured portions are filled with silicone and the raised portions are gently attached to the background to preserve the molded shape.

Making a Repoussé Print. Step 1. The background print is colored, cut, and pasted in place. The skirt of the figure will be stuffed and molded.

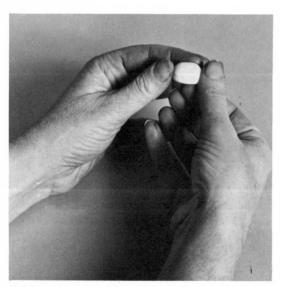

Making a Repoussé Print. Step 2. The bread dough patty which will stuff the print is shaped like a piece of clay. It should not be thicker than ¼''.

Making a Repoussé Print. Step 3. The print to be stuffed is turned over and the patty glued in place.

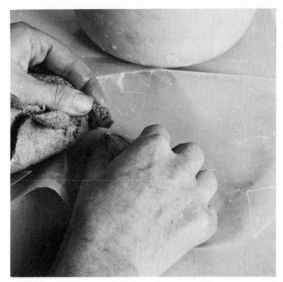

Making a Repoussé Print. Step 4. The print with the glued-in patty is turned face up onto a piece of wax paper. A damp sponge is used to dampen the print and permit molding and shaping with fingers or a soft tool.

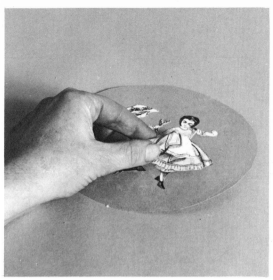

Making a Repoussé Print. Step 5. The print with the stuffing is dried until hard and then glued against the background.

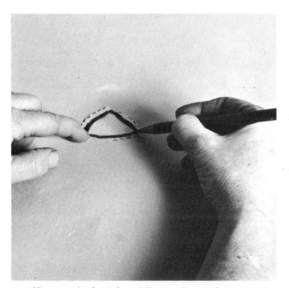

Stuffing a Single Print. When using only one print for stuffed and molded pictures, cut out the part to be stuffed and fill up the hole left in the background print with a piece of tracing paper. Then color in about a ¼" inside the tracing paper "hole" so that the gap left by the raising of the stuffed print will be filled.

Making a Bread Dough Daisy. Step 1. The center of the daisy is made by rolling bread dough the size of a pea and attaching this to floral wire dipped in glue.

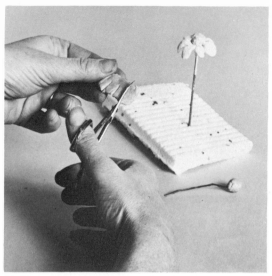

Making a Bread Dough Daisy. Step 2. A piece of bread dough is flattened and nail scissors are used to cut the petal shapes.

Making a Bread Dough Daisy. Step 3. Use your fingers to thin and shape the petals.

Making a Bread Dough Daisy. Step 4. Put a dab of glue around the bottom of the petals and attach them around the center of the daisy.

MOSAIC DECOUPAGE

A mosaic is a design inlaid with small pieces of practically anything. Mosaics have appealed to artists as far back as early Christian and Byzantine times when they were composed of numerous *tesserae* (a Latin word meaning "small pieces") cut from tile, glass, and clay, and the pieces are set in a pattern in cement.

By separating a variety of components in your over-all design and grouping them into separate pictures, framing each with a border so that these "framed designs" make up a series of rectangles and squares, you can create an over-all mosaic pattern to your layout (Figure 62).

Colored papers can be cut into squares, triangles, circles, petals, and diamond shapes and used in a variety of ways. For example, you could have a background inlaid with paper mosaics. While it may seem tedious to handle lots of tiny cutouts, this can be easier than an attempt to paint a two-tone background. With multicolored papers there is no danger of smearing. Decoupage cutouts could be superimposed upon such a mosaic ground.

There are many ways of combining squares, triangles, and circles (Figure 8). These combinations can be used as part of your main decoupage designs and are especially useful as border materials, something a decoupeur always seems to need. If you plan to use lots of these cut shapes, make yourself a cardboard pattern and cut five or six of each shape at one time.

A group of seventh-grade students found the use of mosaic cutouts a most challenging introduction to decoupage. These youngsters showed tremendous imagination in their use of mosaic designs cut out of stamps and colored papers. Typical of a craftsman's ingenuity was their use of a modern hole puncher to cut out tiny circles. Typical of the craftsman's talent for utilizing anything and every-

thing, they saved the punched-out papers to add an interesting note to their backgrounds. The patterns in the diagrams could be used in the same way as the children's designs (Figures 63, 65, and 66).

Special Inlays

In addition to mosaic backgrounds of cut papers, there are several materials which can be used to give a mosaic look to your designs.

Mother-of-pearl flakes. These are obtainable in craft supply stores. They come in variously shaped bits and pieces and, when glued down on a box or pin, work into a natural mosaic pattern. With a little patience you will get the knack of picking up the tiny flakes with a toothpick dipped in water (this works like a magnet) and laying them into a surface covered with glue. Once the flakes are glued down tight, and lightly sanded with dry No. 400 sandpaper, a decoupage design can be superimposed and varnished until it sinks into the mosaic ground (Figure 68).

Eggshells. Used just like mother-of-pearl flakes, eggshells are, of course, no further away than your refrigerator. The technique is very similar: the eggshells are soaked for a day or so in bleach or water to remove the inner membrane. A small piece of eggshell, about the size of a large thumbnail is lightly covered with white glue and pressed, glue-side down, onto the surface. A pushpin or other pointy tool is used to crack the glued-down piece into smaller ones, and move the cracked shells close together with as little space as possible between. This gluing, cracking, and pushing together creates a natural mosaic design. If the background is first painted a dark color, it will show through the cracks and will serve the function of

Figure 62. A round metal desk basket is covered with a "mosaic" of assorted black and white illuminated letters from various periods and sources.

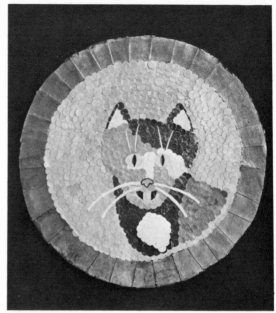

Figure 63. A tiger was done with circles punched out of a hole puncher. Different colors of paper were used to give the tiger shading. Rectangular cutouts are used as a border for this ingenious work of art.

Figure 64. Here is a square wooden box with a "mosaic" of tiny colored pictures.

Figure 65. A decoupage design cut from a Christmas card against a background of gold and silver mosaic circles. Note how the punched-out paper is used to give texture to the wings. Decoupage cut flowers are used for the frame.

Figure 66. Stamps cut into rectangular shapes are laid out to create a fish. Cut papers and punched-out papers were used to create a background that suggests the ocean's depths.

Figure 67. Squares, circles, triangles, and diamond shapes can be combined in an infinite variety of mosaic background and border designs. Those illustrated here are possible combinations.

Figure 68. A trinket box with a mosaic background of mother-of-pearl flakes. The flakes glisten against the figure which is colored green and blue. The flower border is done in red with green accents to match the top design.

79

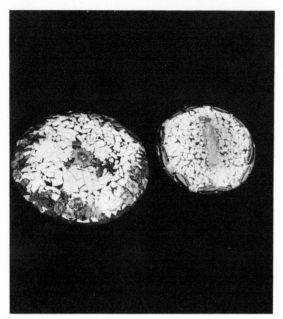

Figure 69. *The pins were made with decoupage designs superimposed upon an eggshell inlay. The small pin is painted red, which shimmers through the eggshell cracks. The larger pin was stained a rich brown.*

Figure 70. *A mosaic owl made up with designs from a baroque scroll.*

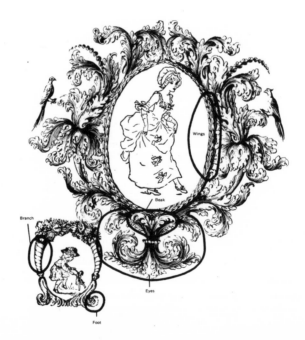

Figure 71. *Prints which suggested feathers for an owl design and scales for a fish design.*

Figure 72. Two decoupage prints suggested this stylish fish, designed on a ground of slate.

Figure 73. Another mosaic fish, the shape suggestion reinforced by the natural fish contour of the driftwood base.

mosaic grouting. Like the mother-of-pearl flakes, the pasted down eggshells are sanded lightly with dry No. 400 sandpaper and the design is then superimposed (Figure 69).

Decoupage Print Mosaics

Sometimes a decoupage print suggests a shape and, instead of using it in the conventional manner, the artist can cut apart the print and use it to fill in a suggested shape. A mosaic owl (Figure 70) was inspired by the "feathery" look of a big scroll (Figure 71). A border pattern suggested the scales of a fish and was beautifully executed on a piece of slate (Figure 72) and again on a piece of driftwood (Figure 73). The driftwood piece underscored the fish design since its contour is like that of a fish.

All sorts of other shapes could have been used instead of the owl and the fish, such as simple birds, human figures, or inanimate objects. The various mosaic materials could be combined just as the fish in the illustrated slate combined "scales" from one border print with a "finlike" border scroll. You could combine petal and round shapes to go with various shapes within the figure you are filling in. For example, round circles could have been used for the owl's eyes, diamond shapes for the body, and triangles for the feet and ears.

It is very good training to study basic shapes in terms of arranging them into various patterns. Look at conventional decoupage materials in terms of finding suggestions for feathers, eyes, and things that are not immediately obvious. As those famous masters of comic operetta, Gilbert and Sullivan, so aptly put it: "Things are never as they seem, skim milk masquerades as cream" (*H.M.S. Pinafore, Act II.*) Let us examine one of these illustrated mosaics to see how a baroque scroll was made to masquerade as a gay owl.

Making a Mosaic Owl Plaque

The outline of the owl to be filled in with a decoupage design is drawn freehand or traced from a picture. A children's coloring book can provide the outline for all sorts of usable mosaic bases for the decoupeur. The childish look of your base outline does not matter. You will be filling in the details with more subtly colored designs.

The drawn outline should be cut together with a piece of heavy cardboard or cork which can serve as a ready-to-hang shaped backing. You could also use a shaped background of self-hardening clay. Simply roll a ball of clay into a slab about ¼" thick. Dip a sharp knife into water and, using your paper pattern as a guide, cut out a clay owl. When this has hardened you can paint it and glue your designs to the clay owl. There will be more about working with clay in Chapters 8 and 9.

Study your print carefully (Figure 71) to see what you will need to make up your mosaic. Save the round parts for the eyes. Look for some pointy bits of print for the ears. In the illustrated print the big swirly portions were quite obviously going to make up the owl's feathers. The swirls at the bottom seemed to suggest eyes and eyebrows; plain circles of colored paper could have been used instead. The little cartouches at the bottom of the print looked sort of woodlike and thus provided a perching branch.

Once it was decided which parts of the print would be used to flesh out the owl, the scrolls could be colored. In the illustrated owl the feathers were colored with orange pencil in the shaded spots. Yellow was blended all over for a rich, golden look. The beak, feet, and feathers were colored in brown and gold. The inner rim of the scroll, which served as the owl's wings, was colored in brown and yellow.

After the designs were colored and sprayed with sealer, they were cut apart and pasted in. The pasting in this case involved a certain amount of overlapping of print edges but this actually added to the texture and dimension. A traditionally ridgeless, supersmooth finish would have been less desirable. (See the Demonstration on making a mosaic owl at the end of the chapter.)

Since the designs do overlap and the usual finish is not possible, finishing should be done with a quick process, with emphasis on protection and sheen rather than elegant patina. You could coat your design with two or three coats of acrylic polymer gloss medium, which can be found in art supply stores. This will give you a textured type of finish and require no rubbing at all. You could also finish off your piece with seven or eight coats of lacquer finish. The finish should be sanded with No. 400 and No. 600 sandpaper only, then steel-wooled and waxed. The illustrated owl was finished.

Study the owl and the fish made from the prints and then look through your own prints and see if there are any interesting animals lurking among the scrolls and borders. Study the stamp and hole-punched circle designs and see if you can come up with some colored paper and stamp mosaics of your own. While none of this is decoupage in the conventional sense of the word, it is an interesting way to depart from the traditional materials.

Demonstration

Making a Mosaic Owl. *You can see here how colored and cut designs can be pasted onto the owl-shaped background. Notice that, unlike "regular" decoupage, design edges can be allowed to touch or overlap.*

Figure 74. *(Above) A tailored box bought in bisque state from a ceramics studio. The box was painted blue and decorated with an equestrian theme. The inside was painted white, and also done with decoupage designs.*

Figure 75. *(Right) A pencil holder made from a fat slab of clay which was shaped to fit the illustration from an old magazine. Pencils were used to dig out the holes. The pencil holder's side and rear designs consisted of old patent medicine ads.*

CERAMIC DECOUPAGE

The pottery you see in stores and galleries has usually been subject to two firing processes in a ceramic kiln. The first firing is called biscuit firing. It hardens the potter's shape into what is called bisque (pronounced "bisk") ware. The ceramic artist glazes his bisque ware and fires this glaze into the pottery during a second firing.

Simple Glazed Pottery

You can take a piece of pottery with a very simple glaze finish and decoupage right on top of this. Working on top of glazed pottery is very simple since you eliminate the steps of sanding and painting.

Unglazed Pottery

You can apply your decoupage cutouts to unglazed ceramics or bisque ware. Instead of finishing with glaze, you paint your bisque item, as you would any decoupage. This finish will serve to waterproof and make the item as durable as a second firing would (Figure 74). Ceramic-teaching studios have mushroomed throughout the country. They have molds of popular shapes so that you can buy a large variety of plaques, boxes, and pots. You will find at least one such studio listed in your telephone directory under "Ceramics." The studio owner will expect you to come in two times. The first time you pick out the shape you want. It will be in a soft or greenware stage, having been poured into a mold, but not yet fired in a kiln. The studio owner will ask you to clean up your greenware or will do it for you at a nominal cost. Your piece will then be fired in the studio kiln to bisque state. At this point, you come to pick it up.

Ceramic Making

You can use ceramics as another opportunity to create a total craft; by making your own shapes, you can create *and* decorate the surface. Like papier-mâché, ceramics is an old and honored art and lends itself ideally to decoupage.

You need no access to a pottery-throwing wheel or kiln to become acquainted with ceramic decoupage. All the projects demonstrated and illustrated here were made with self-hardening clay, by the slab-building method. Self-hardening clay is available in any art or hobby supply store and hardens when exposed to air. Some self-hardening clays can be baked slowly in a kitchen oven. This type of clay is worked and handled exactly like clay which would be fired. If you become interested in exploring ceramics further, you can go right into a ceramics class with what you have learned here as your background.

If you live near a studio which is willing to biscuit fire your hand-built clay for you (most commercial studios will fire only molded ware), or if you have access to a school or community center kiln, you can, of course, use the regular firing clays which are somewhat less expensive and which are preferred by ceramics lovers.

By making your own ceramic base and decorating it with decoupage rather than a glaze, you will be creating a very unique piece of art which defies comparison with other forms of pottery. From the ceramist's point of view, self-hardening clay has too smooth a finish. If such a piece is finished with paint, it can never quite compare with a piece of fired and glazed pottery. However, the decoupage finish is perfect for the very smooth clay surface and the hand varnishing and rubbing will give a finish that is lovely to look at and feel.

Once you begin to work with a hunk of clay, something will happen to your creative perception. Experiments with different shapes will inspire you with new ways to design. I hope you will find, as I did, that a closer and more meaningful relationship between surface and surface decorating will ensue, along with a general freeing of your artistic spirit.

Pottery-Making Methods

There are several methods of making pottery.

The coil method. Roll out sausages of clay, then build one upon the other. The coil lines are smoothed out as the object is built up. This is one of the oldest techniques; it was often used by the Indians. In ceramic decoupage you will be using coils to reinforce the insides of boxes.

Modeling. Another method of building with clay is to take a chunk of clay and pinch, pull, and slap it into the basic shape you want, then pare and hollow where needed (Figure 75).

Slab building. For our purposes, this is the ideal method. It involves rolling the clay into slabs which are then cut and joined to achieve a desired shape. Practically any object can be made by the slab-building technique. It is the simplest method for beginners and it is upon this method that we will concentrate in this chapter and the next.

Materials for Making Ceramic Bases

The following items are required for ceramic making.

Self-hardening clay. A five-pound package will allow you to complete all the step-by-step demonstrations in this chapter and the next. If you are going to have your ceramic ware fired, check with the person doing the firing as to which type of clay is best for his kiln.

Sponge. Used damp to smooth the clay down. Also, a damp sponge will keep unused clay moist and pliable if sealed in a plastic bag with the clay.

Pointed knife. To cut and rough up edges.

Pointy tools. Knitting needles, awls, toothpicks, or nails can be used to make hanging holes.

Brush. An inexpensive ½" brush will be used to smooth clay.

Dropcloth. Lots of newspapers, a large piece of oilcloth with a textured back, or burlap.

Sticks. Two wooden sticks, ½" thick, can be used to control the thickness of the clay.

Roller. A household rolling pin or a heavy dowel stick is used to roll out clay.

Preparing Clay

Knead your clay to make it soft and pliable. It is always somewhat hard when first taken out of the package. Throw the clay down on your working surface to get out some of the excess moisture. When working with self-hardening clay this is all the preparation your clay needs.

Clay which will be fired in a ceramic kiln needs more careful preparation. The kneading must be done for quite some time (about fifteen minutes) to be sure that you get out all the air bubbles. Instead of kneading you could throw the clay down on a hard surface and cut it in half until the two halves of the cut clay are absolutely smooth and free of air bubbles. The two halves are then put together again and the process (known as wedging) is repeated. A definite advantage of self-hardening clay is that you do not have to worry about whether or not you have wedged properly.

It will take some practice to roll nice even slabs. Slabs approximately ¼" thick are ideal and the guiding sticks on either side of your clay will be very helpful for getting the feel of correct thickness.

Preparing and Joining Forms

You can cut cardboard or paper patterns for bottoms, sides, lids, and bases to help you cut out better-fitting slabs. Be sure always to dip your knife into water before cutting clay.

You don't have to worry about "slip," the potter's term for a soft wet clay used as a form of cement. If you dip your brush generously into water and brush into the sections to be joined, you will create your own.

As long as you keep your work covered with a damp cloth or plastic bag, it will remain soft enough for you to trim and pare and make adjustments. Once you are completely satisfied, you can expose your piece to the air for complete drying.

Drying

Before your clay reaches its final stage of hardness it will reach a point where it feels like leather. It is during this leather-hard stage that final adjustments can be made and bumps and imperfections smoothed out. If you use a smooth stone or the back of a spoon to rub your surface, there will be little need to sand or rasp when the clay is completely hard. However, the clay *can* be sanded or rasped when the clay is completely hard. This stone smoothing gives a polished look to bisque-fired ware which almost looks like a glaze.

Painting

Your hardened clay can be painted with any type of paint. I find the nonfiring stains put out by ceramic supply companies particularly good, attractive, and inexpensive. Ceramic studios carry both water- and petroleum-based finishes. They can also be used for surfaces other than clay. Before painting with *any* paint you should seal your clay with one or two light coats of clear plastic spray.

Now that we have talked about working with clay in a general way, let's make some specific objects which will be suitable for decoupage designs and which offer you a basis for working out a variety of other clay objects.

Making a Clay Flower Holder

This is a very attractive and simple basic item. The holder can be enlarged to be used as a letter holder. The flower-holding pocket can be partially sealed to turn it into a pencil holder. The back portion of the holder alone can be enlarged and changed in shape to make just about any type of hanging plaque. You will be working with two slabs of clay.

Preparing the Slabs

Roll out a slab large enough so that you can cut both the back and pocket slabs needed to make the flower holder at one time. Dip your knife into water and cut out the shapes, cutting either free form or with a cardboard pattern. Sponge your slab smooth, both on top and around the edges. (See the Demonstration on making a clay flower holder, *Steps 1, 2, and 3*, at the end of the chapter.)

Curve the pocket part of your slab. It will not break. If any little cracks appear, you need only to dip your sponge in water and smooth them out. Hold the curved slab against the straight one to test the shape. (See the Demonstration on making

a clay flower holder, *Step 4*, at the end of the chapter.)

Joining the Pieces

To join the pocket to the back portion of the holder, dip your knife in water and make little zigzag marks all around the edges of the curved slab, and all around the portions of the flat slab where the pocket will touch. (See the Demonstration on making a clay flower holder, *Step 5*, at the end of the chapter.) This is called roughing up the surface. Without this roughing up of surfaces there is nothing for your clay to grip onto during the joining process.

Dip your brush in water and drip water into the grooved, roughed-up sections. By making this all wet and mushy, you are creating your own slip or clay cement.

Now press the wet, roughed-up portion together. Hold your finger inside the pocket to keep the curve. Keep brushing the outside edges with the wet brush. You can also use your fingers and/or the sponge to smooth down the edges and keep working the joined sections together. When the outside sections are solidly together, take your wet brush and work it around the inside of the pocket to complete the welding. (See the Demonstration on making a clay flower holder, *Steps 6 and 7*, at the end of the chapter.)

Smooth everything down with your wet sponge.

Use a nail or other pointed tool to make a hole at the top and bottom of the back part of the holder. Dip the drilling tool into water. These holes will be your hangers. (See the Demonstration on making a clay flower holder, *Step 8*, at the end of the chapter.)

Drying

Your flower holder should lie flat during drying. If you have a piece of Masonite, the rough pebbly side of this makes an excellent surface upon which to rest and dry the clay.

Keep a plastic bag, open at one end, over the piece to let it dry slowly and give you a chance to make any adjustments in the shape.

When you are satisfied with the piece, you can remove the plastic cover and let it air dry. Keep it near a bright window for natural sun heat.

As soon as your clay feels leather hard, use the back of a spoon or a stone to smooth the surface. You can smooth further with sandpaper or a rasp

Figure 76. One of the special joys of creating one's own objects is the total appropriateness of a shape. This heart, for example, is ideally suited to the romantic theme of lovebirds and a pair of human lovers. A dainty gold paper trim decorates the sides. The flesh tones look lovely against a royal blue (See Color Plate 12.)

Figure 77. Remember the mosaic owl from Chapter 6? Here it is again as a flower or pencil holder, with the new dimension afforded by the ceramic repoussé technique. The owl base was painted a cherry red with contrasting reds and pinks. (See Color Plate 15.)

when the clay is completely hard. (See the Demonstration on making a clay flower holder, *Steps 9 and 10*, at the end of the chapter.)

Making a Box

Making a box will carry you a step beyond the flower holder. Not only will you be joining two parts together, but you will have to make a lid which will fit the bottom of the box.

The illustrated box is made from an oval base which is not only attractive but enables you to make a side from a single slab. A round or heart-shaped box (Figure 76) could also be made this way. A square or rectangular box is best made with four separate side pieces.

Preparing the Slabs

You will need a slab large enough to cut out the top and bottom and the long side slab. The same pattern could be used since top and bottom will be the same size. (See the Demonstration on making a clay box, *Step 1*, at the end of the chapter.)

Lay your cardboard pattern on the rolled-out clay. With a wet knife cut around the pattern.

Joining the Pieces

The side of the box is joined to the box bottom just as the pocket was joined to the back of the flower holder. The edges of both the box bottom and of the side slab are roughed up. Water is worked into these roughed-up surfaces with the brush to create the welding slip. The side is pressed firmly against the bottom and end parts are joined where they meet. (See the Demonstration on making a clay box, *Steps 2 and 3*, at the end of the chapter.) Be sure these joined ends are also roughed up and wet down with slip.

To reinforce the bottom of the box, roll out a thin sausage of clay. (See the Demonstration on making a clay box, *Step 4*, at the end of the chapter.) Rough it up with your wet knife and weld it all around the inside of the box.

Making the Box Lid

Instead of attaching sides as you did to the bottom oval, you will be attaching a rim to your oval lid. This is made just as you made the reinforcement for the bottom, only you will need a thicker coil, a coil about ¼" to ½" thick makes a good inner rim.

Rough up the coil and the portion of the rim where it will join and weld together. (See the Demonstration on making a clay box, *Step 5*, at the end of the chapter.)

Allow the lid to dry on its back, with the rim face up until it gets leather hard. When the lid is leather hard, fit it into the box (if you do this earlier, your rim is going to come off and your lid will lose its shape). You will still be able to trim or pare off any little imperfections or protrusions. (See the Demonstration on making a clay box, *Step 6*, at the end of the chapter.) Let the box continue to dry with the cover in place to insure the perfect fit.

Working Around a Mold

Ceramists use all sorts of molds to achieve interesting and original shapes. A glass might serve as a mold for a canister or a large rock for a more abstract shape. A mold serves as a support while the clay is being formed and while it is still very soft. As soon as the clay becomes leathery, the mold is pulled away since the clay can now stand free by itself.

One of the easiest and most versatile molds available is a balloon. Blow it up to the size you want, cut your slab pieces to fit around the mold, and, as soon as the clay becomes leather hard, gently let the air out of the balloon and pull it out. You will have a perfect hollow. This is especially important if you fire clay in a kiln, where beginners' projects often explode because they have not been properly hollowed.

Making a Balloon-Mold Pot

Blow up a small balloon. Leave enough of an end to pull it out by when you are ready to release the air. Then, use the balloon to make a pattern on paper. This will look like a four-leafed daisy, with the center or sitting portion of the balloon a small circle, and four petals which will be joined as the sides of the pot. (See the Demonstration on makng a balloon-mold pot, *Step 1*, at the end of the chapter.)

Roll out a slab large enough to accommodate your paper pattern. Once you are experienced with this method, you can skip the pattern and make your outline directly on the rolled-out clay slab. Cut out your basic slab and sit the balloon in its center. Now join the sides together one by one: rough up each side, make slip, then press firmly together. You will find that the balloon has a nice "give" which enables you to mold and seam your sides together easily. The balloon will not burst because the wet clay holds it. (See the Demonstration on making a balloon-mold pot, *Step 2*, at the end of the chapter.)

When all the sides are joined, sponge the whole pot smooth, erasing all the joining marks. Then, allow the pot to dry until the clay becomes leathery. Deflate your balloon by stabbing a hole with a needle and letting the air out. Since the balloon will have expanded inside the wet clay, the deflating process will take some time. Do not rush. The balloon *should* come out slowly. Eventually you will be able to pull out the deflated balloon. You can then trim the pot's neck and shape it to your liking. Later, when the pot is completely hard you can smooth and shape some more with a rasp. (See the Demonstration on making a balloon-mold pot, *Steps 3, 4, and 5*, at the end of the chapter.)

Ceramic Repoussé

One of the most exciting aspects of using new methods in decoupage is that one innovation leads to another. What I like to call ceramic repoussé is a perfect example of this.

When to Use Ceramic Repoussé

A fruit design lends itself particularly well to sculpturing and so, if you were to make a clay container which you planned to decorate with fruit designs, you would make a canister to accommodate your design and put in two bumps in the spots to be covered by the fruits (Figure 78).

If you planned to do an owl, it would be possible to make two bumps where the eyes would go and another one for the beak and thus create a more interesting bird (Figure 77).

This method of achieving a third dimension by incorporating the raised effect into the ceramic background works best with a simple design where there will be no great displacement of the print. Fruits, full costumes, and plumed birds are suitable designs. They should not be connected to a lot of other material in the design or you will create problems in the design.

Stuffing With Clay

When stuffing a print in the conventional way, the stuffing is usually quite thin. However, clay pro-

Figure 78. Here is a canister decorated with a fruit design which is given more dimension by means of ceramic repoussé.

Figure 79. The repoussé fish plaque is shown complete from our step-by-step demonstration. The plaque is a pale blue color and the border designs are in bluish greens and dark blues. The fish is in a grayish blue. The whole design is in keeping with basic sea colors and forms.

vides a fatter bump, about ½" thick at the center, narrowing down at the edges. Since such a fat bump tends to "shrink" the print because much of it will have to be molded and curved, it is best to work with a print that is not so small that it will get lost in the raising process. The illustrated owl did not have large designs, but this presented no problem since the mosaic designs were worked around, rather than over, the eye bumps and the beak was make up of several separate little pieces.

A fish is an excellent subject for this sort of stuffing. Let us see how this would work out step-by-step.

Making a Ceramic Repoussé Fish

A plaque large enough to permit additional flat decoupage designing seems an ideal background. A small plate serves as a pattern for cutting a perfect circle out of a slab of clay. Then, a clay patty is formed in the palm of the hand and tried out under the cut-out paper fish for size. The patty should be smaller than the paper design by about ¼". It can be ½" thick at the center, narrowing down to ¼" at the edges.

The flat side of the patty and the portion of the plaque where it will be joined must be roughed up for proper joining. Then, a little water is brushed onto both roughed-up surfaces and joined and smoothed down. (See the Demonstration on making a repoussé fish, *Steps 1 and 2*, at the end of the chapter.)

The plaque must be thoroughly dry and painted before the fish and other designs are placed.

Placing the Design

To mold the fish over the bump which will be very hard and will not have the give of the bread dough, it is best to make several slits all around the design so that it will move and conform around the raised bump without tearing or wrinkling. As you paste the design down, these slits will move together and will not show in the finished design (Figure 79). (See the Demonstration on making a repoussé fish, *Steps 3 and 4*, at the end of the chapter.)

Making a Clay Flower Holder. Step 1. Roll a slab for the two pieces needed to make a flower holder.

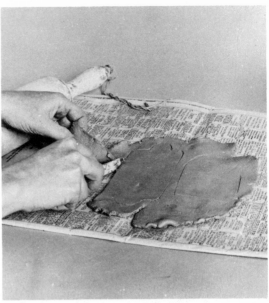

Making a Clay Flower Holder. Step 2. The design outline is scratched in with the tip of the knife and cut out. Knife must always be dipped in water before cutting.

Making a Clay Flower Holder. Step 3. The wet sponge is used to smooth down surface and edges of the cut slabs.

Making a Clay Flower Holder. Step 4. The pocket portion of the flower holder is curved up.

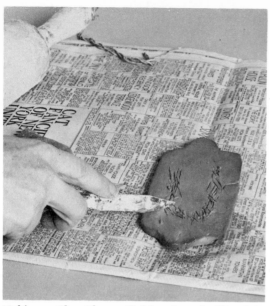

Making a Clay Flower Holder. Step 5. The slabs are roughed up in preparation for joining.

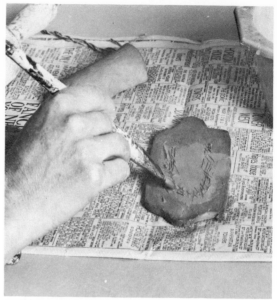

Making a Clay Flower Holder. Step 6. A brush is dipped in water and water is dripped onto the roughed-up clay to create slip, which acts like a glue.

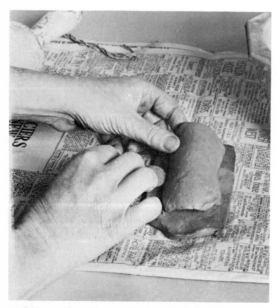

Making a Clay Flower Holder. Step 7. The pocket, its edges also roughed up, is welded to the back portion of the holder. Fingers and sponge should be used to keep smoothing at the joined sections until all joining marks disappear and the attachment is solid.

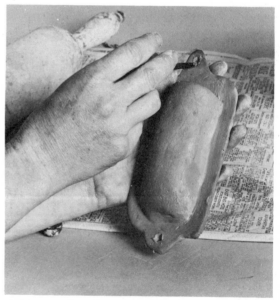

Making a Clay Flower Holder. Step 8. A pointed tool is used to make holes for hanging the holder.

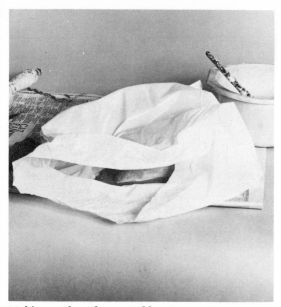

Making a Clay Flower Holder. *Step 9. The finished piece is dried slowly under a plastic bag to allow alterations and adjustments.*

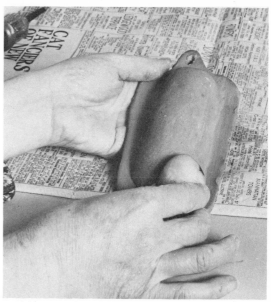

Making a Clay Flower Holder. *Step 10. The leather-hardened clay is smoothed with a stone. When solidly hard, it can be further smoothed with sandpaper or a rasp.*

Making a Clay Box. *Step 1. The clay slab must be large enough to allow for three patterns to be cut from it.*

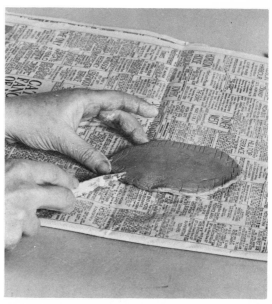

Making a Clay Box. *Step 2. The bottom of the box is roughed up in preparation for joining with the sides. A brush and water are for making slip.*

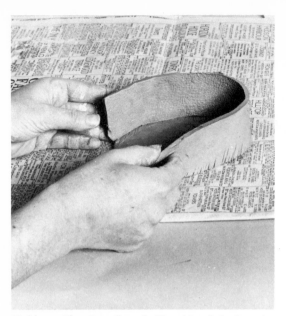

Making a Clay Box. Step 3. The side of the box, its joining edges roughed up, is welded to the bottom and joined where the two ends meet.

Making a Clay Box. Step 4. A welding sausage of clay is put inside the box bottom as a reinforcement.

Making a Clay Box. Step 5. A rim, which is just a fatter version of the welding sausage, is attached to the box lid.

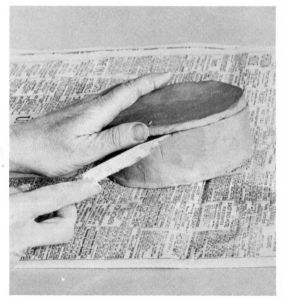

Making a Clay Box. Step 6. When the box is leather hard, the lid is tried on for fit. Any unevenness can be trimmed with a knife at this point. The box should continue to dry with the lid in place.

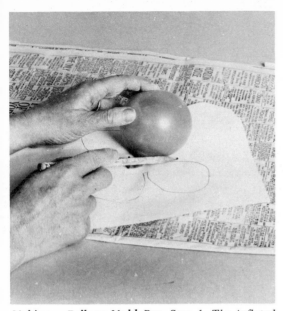

Making a Balloon-Mold Pot. Step 1. The inflated balloon is used to outline a paper pattern for the basic pot slab.

Making a Balloon-Mold Pot. Step 2. The balloon is placed in the center of the cut-out slab and each section is joined.

Making a Balloon-Mold Pot. Step 3. When the clay hardens, the balloon is slowly pulled out.

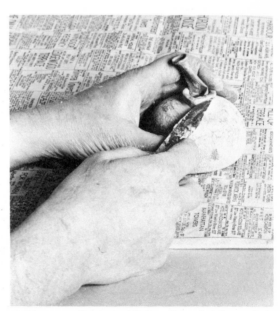

Making a Balloon-Mold Pot. Step 4. The neck is trimmed and shaped. It could also be widened (Figure 84).

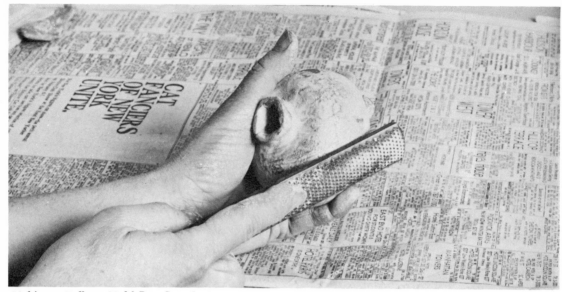

Making a Balloon-Mold Pot. Step 5. A rasp is used to smooth and shape the contours of the pot.

Making a Repoussé Fish. Step 1. The clay plaque all cut out, with a hanging hole put in. A clay patty is tested under the central fish design.

Making a Repoussé Fish. Step 2. The flat part of the patty is roughed up; so is the portion of the plaque to which it will be joined.

Making a Repoussé Fish. Step 3. When the plaque has dried completely and has been painted, the fish is ready to be molded over the clay bump. To avoid tearing and wrinkling, slits are made, the scissors cutting into shading lines to hide all marks.

Making a Repoussé Fish. Step 4. The fish is glued over the bump and the loose parts make the molding process very easy. If you carefully press them down and together, no lines will show.

CERAMIC DECOUPAGE JEWELRY

Since time immemorial man has used jewelry as an expression of his love of personal adornment. Look through any illustrated history book or at paintings of men and women of other eras and civilizations and you will see finger rings and earrings, pins, pendants, brooches, bracelets, and a whole miscellany of personal adornments.

Historically, gold was one of the chief materials used in ornament, mainly because it was always available in its natural state in all parts of the world. Eventually, other metals were hammered and molded to the craftsman's need. Today, the variety of materials used to fashion jewelry is too large to enumerate.

Materials

Fine jewelry is made out of precious metals and stones. Costume jewelry uses less costly materials. As a decoupeur, you can create a piece of costume jewelry which is distinctive and original, much less subject to the tides of fashion than commercially produced jewelry. We have already discussed the possibility of pins, pendants, and rings made out of wood (Chapter 3), stones (Chapter 4), and papier-mâché (Chapter 5). By fashioning your jewelry on a ceramic base and decorating it with decoupage designs, you have the opportunity for a new creative adventure. As with the boxes and containers fashioned in the last chapter, you need no special ceramic equipment. Self-hardening clay is particularly suitable for jewelry and the method of rolling out slabs and cutting them into suitable shapes is adaptable to all your needs.

Design Ideas

Design ideas are as limitless as the base shapes. Interesting letters are marvelous for monogram designs. Favorite flowers, hobbies, animals are easy to find and you will only need a few cutting materials for these small items. A symbolic sort of design, such as clasped hands for friendship, zodiac signs, state flowers, meaningful words such as "Love" and "Peace," all lend themselves to ceramic decoupage jewelry. Once you get going, I am sure you will have difficulty in keeping up with your ideas.

If you are interested in the profitable aspect of decoupage, jewelry is one of your best bets. The items are small, easy, and faster to make than most decoupage. The combination of ceramics and decoupage works especially well. Clay must be worked thick and large enough to prevent cracking, and decoupage calls for a surface large enough to permit an interesting design. If you do decide to do a great deal of this ceramic decoupage jewelry, you could buy a very small kiln which heats up just enough for biscuit firing but is not large enough or hot enough for glazing. These kilns are very inexpensive. I have one which was given to me by a dentist who used to use it to make individual teeth! The kiln is not a must, however, and all the samples in this chapter were made with self-hardening clay.

Jewelry Findings

The materials used for jewelry must be adaptable to a way of wearing them. Thus, you need to know something about mechanical fittings or findings. There are findings available for every type and shape of jewelry. The designer of fine, rather than costume, jewelry prefers to work with top-quality metal chains and links. However, the costume jeweler, especially a beginner, can obtain inexpensive and very useful findings made of yellow or white metal-plated brass or nickel.

Figure 80. *A pair of mushrooms on a base make a unique ceramic item. Flowers seem to be climbing all around the mushroom, and the unusual butterfly dancing girls are shaped perfectly for the mushroom caps. The colors are pastel blues, greens, and pinks against an eggshell white.*

Figure 81. *Any type of plaque can be made once you know how to roll out a clay slab. Here is a beauty-plus-utility idea: a switchplate. The flowers and butterflies from* Ladies' Amusement *seem just made for its shape. (See Color Plate 4.)*

Figure 82. *Here is the flower holder from our step-by-step demonstration, painted a chrome yellow, and designed with figures from an old bookplate. Handmade bread dough daisies fill the holder.*

Since the type of decoupage described in this book usually combines these metal findings with nontypical jewelry materials—wood, papier-mâché, ceramics—your choice of findings will be based upon what will adhere easily to these particular surfaces. We will need bellcaps wide enough to open around stones, pinbacks, and rings which can be glued rather than soldered. Ordinary light-weight wire sold on little rolls in a hardware store can be used to string beads and to fashion whatever is not readily available. The suppliers listed at the back of the book will all ship small orders, unlike many dealers who supply only by the gross lot.

Necklaces, earrings, pins, pendants, finger rings, bracelets, and hair ornaments are the chief categories of jewelry. Let us now take a look at how some of these would be worked out in terms of a ceramic base with decoupage designs.

Pins

This is one of the simplest and most versatile types of ceramic jewelry you can create. Since you want to be able to decorate your pin with an interesting design, this should have at least a 2" surface. Shapes can be round or geometric. Natural forms such as leaves, animals, human, or artificial are extremely suitable.

Making a Pin

Roll out a slab of clay. If you plan to make several pins, you can cut a number of pins out of the same slab. Use a cardboard pattern or cut your pin free-form. Be sure to dip your cutting knife in water. You can use any hard-edged object as a cutting guide.

Use a damp sponge to smooth the surface and to soften the edges. If you look at a finished pin you will notice that if it is well shaped, it thins down somewhat at the edges. By sponging gently but firmly you can achieve curved, round edges which will be more attractive than a completely level look. In the clover-shaped pin (Figure 85), the leaves were gently indented with a wet thumb. The surface was still smooth enough to take well to a decoupage design, but this slight indentation gave a more fluid look.

Take the pinback which you will be using to hold your pin and use it to make an indentation into the back of the moist clay. You will not be cementing the pinback to the pin until the clay has

Figure 83. The box is shown in its final stage from the step-by-step box demonstration. The background is a brilliant green. The lid design shows a scene depicting peace and plenty, with figures colored in blues and yellows. As you can see, the peace and plenty theme is carried through on the sides, enclosed in an oval of daisies. Everything—shape, color, and design—truly works in this completely handmade decoupage.

Figure 84. Here is a pot which was shaped around a balloon. It has a primitive charm because its shape is not perfect. The background was painted a ceramic stain of terra cotta, with a wood stain wiped in. The oriental designs are taken from an old encyclopedia and are colored in blue-greens and rust-reds.

Figure 85. A pin shaped like a clover leaf. The background is bright green, the designs black and white.

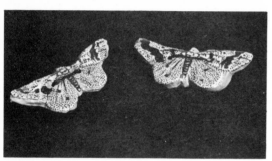

Figure 86. For a special accent, make butterfly buttons with matching butterfly designs.

Figure 87. The initial E has been carved into the clay pendant and the decoupage designs are all tiny illustrations of objects starting with this letter. The pendant is a beige-gold, the grooves are rubbed with gold.

hardened and been painted, but with this indentation worked into the back, the pin will fit and hold much better. This step is essential with any type of finding which will be cemented on after the clay has hardened and is painted. (See the Demonstration on making a pin at the end of the chapter.)

Making Buttons

In ancient times pins were used not just as ornaments but also to secure garments (as we use buttons nowadays). Keeping this in mind, you might want to enhance a garment by using your pins in a utilitarian as well as decorative way. In that case, instead of attaching a pinback finding, you would use a toothpick or thin nail to make two holes in the center of the button. Your problem in designing will be that you have to work around the line of thread which will run from hole to hole after you have sewn your button into place on the garment.

Another problem which presents itself is that such buttons must not be dry cleaned or washed. For this reason I would recommend that you make buttons for items which need a minimum of dry cleaning. For example, two butterfly-shaped ceramic buttons provided a nice fashion note for a vest. The buttons were shaped to fit the finished design and there was very little need for varnishing since the paper and ceramic edges were in line. Where a print is mounted on a shape of matching proportions as on the vest buttons, you are creating more of a montage than a decoupage (Figure 86).

In general, make buttons as regular pins to that they can be easily moved from garment to garment.

Pendants

Pendants have been made since the days of oldest antiquity. They are most commonly attached to neck chains and suspended from one point. This makes them especially intriguing in terms of a two-faced design. Pendants, like pins, can take many shapes. If you plan your design ahead of time, you can coordinate it with the base shape. For example, a group of tiny religious scenes might fit onto a large cross. A monogram might be grooved out with a toothpick or nail to accommodate tiny illustrations in keeping with that monogram (Figure 87).

Making a Pendant

To make a pendant, first roll out your clay slab and cut out the desired shape. Then, use a pointed tool dipped in water to make a hanging hole. This should be close to the top, but be careful that it is not so close to the edge that it will crack when you add your attachment.

While the clay is still wet, make any patterns or indentations you will need to accommodate your design. Groove out an initial, or press in an indentation for a stone or a mirror which you might want to glue in to be surrounded by a decoupage "frame" (Figure 88).

To hang your pendant, you could pass your chain right through the hole you have made. Some chains are too thick so have a large jewelry finding known as a jump ring handy. Jump rings come in all sizes. For a ceramic piece, you should have one which measures at least ¼". You could fashion your own jump ring by cutting a piece off a one-ounce wire spool available at the hardware store. Pull this wire through the hole, and twist tightly into a loop through which your chain can be pulled without difficulty.

Figure 88. The other side of the initial pendant is shown here. A mirror was pasted into an indented spot which was made while the clay was wet. The frame is decorated with a shower of roses.

Ceramic Rings

Rings, more than any other type of jewelry, have always been worn by both men and women. They range from the purely ornamental to the symbolic. The current popularity of rings is reminiscent of the Renaissance, when several finger rings on each hand were the mark of the distinguished, well-dressed aristocrat, who undoubtedly wore beautiful rings done in decoupage.

The decoupeur who loved the chunky style of the rock rings described in Chapter 4 will find further excitement in making a ceramic ring base. The friendship design of clasped hands within a circlet of flowers (Figure 41) can now be underscored by the romantic base shape of a heart (Figure 89). Triangle, diamond, abstract, and realistic shapes can all be rolled out in minutes. Since a clay ring band would be rather thick and awkward, it is advisable to attach your clay shape to a ring base from a jewelry supplier. This base should have a flat top to which you will cement the hardened piece of clay. While cementing should be saved until the clay is hard, the shape of the ring base should be indented into the wet clay. (See the Demonstration on making a pin at the end of the chapter.)

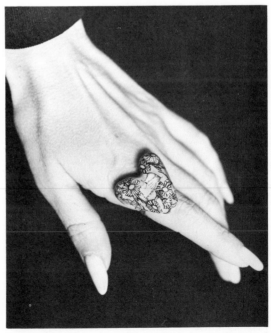

Figure 89. Here is a ring which is symbolic of friendship and love from its heart-shaped base to its daisy-encircled clasped hands.

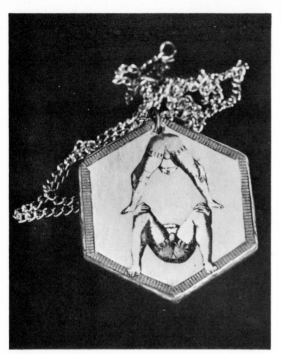

Figure 90. *Pendants and pins can take any shape when you make your own base out of clay. A hexagon shape seemed particularly appropriate for a design of acrobats surrounded by a tailored border. The other side is designed with a horse and rider, a perfect gift for a youngster who is interested in sports.*

Figure 91. *Here is the finished barrette from our demonstration of draping over a hump mold balloon. The terra cotta background would blend well with any hair coloring. The Roman scroll is colored to blend with the background.*

Cufflinks and Tiepins

Men's jewelry specialties such as cufflinks and tiepins could be fashioned in a similar manner. You roll out a square or round shape and cement it to the top of a flat, ready-made, inexpensive cufflink. In the case of a tieclip, the conventional shape is usually rectangular and should be made as large as possible for purposes of your decoupage design. Again, it would be cemented to an inexpensive, flat, ready-made tiebar complete with the clip-on attachment. Both these items are listed in jewelry findings catalogs.

Hair Ornaments

Combs, tiaras, and other hair clasps have long served the dual purpose of adornment and utility. With long hair more popular than ever, a hair barrette is a fashionable and useful accessory. To make a barrette out of clay, it is important to create a shape that will not be too flat or too curved, otherwise, it will not conform to the shape of the head. One of the easiest ways to achieve a soft curve is to create a barrette over a hump mold.

A hump mold is a shape, or hump, over which your clay is draped. It is not joined or sealed. Dishes, rocks, all sorts of bases, can serve as hump molds. For a barrette, we found a balloon to be a perfect hump mold since it has enough "give" to allow draping and contouring.

Making a Barrette

Cut a circle from a slab of clay. This particular item lends itself to free-form cutting rather than a rigid pattern. Cut out an inner rim through which the hair will be pulled. Then, drape your clay barrette over a balloon hump mold. (See the Demonstration on making a barrette at the end of the chapter.) If the balloon does not stay in place, put it inside a dish.

When the clay is leather hard pull it away from the mold and allow it to harden. A wooden twig can be sanded and painted to match the barrette. This will be the pin to hold the hair.

Necklaces

Necklaces of many materials and variations have always been favored by women the world over. When working with ceramic decoupage, antique designs offer the most interesting opportunities for striking artistic effects. By stringing together a series of pendants a collar is formed around the neck. The collar necklace and matching earrings illustrated in our step-by-step demonstration might have been worn by the fourteenth-century Egyptian Queen Nefertiti, but would look equally well on a twentieth-century woman. Before we go into detailed demonstration steps for making an Egyptian collar necklace and earrings, let's look at some of the jewelry materials you will need:

Jewelry Materials

Here are some of the materials you should have for jewelry making.

Snips. For cutting chains and wire (the wire is often so lightweight that it could be cut with a good strong scissors).

Pointed pliers. For opening and closing jump rings and catches. The large jump rings suggested for the pendants could be opened with agile hands or eyebrow tweezers, but when your jewelry involves several attachment steps, the pliers and snips will come in handy.

Wire. A roll of one-ounce wire for stringing your necklace pieces together.

Jump rings. To connect the wire with the closing chain for the necklace and to connect the earrings with earring wires.

Earring wire. Either pierced or screwback, depending on your preference.

Necklace chain. This is sold by the inch and comes in all finishes. You will need 1" or 2" for your necklace closing and you might add 1" to your earrings if you want them to drop really low.

A safety catch. For closing the necklace.

The snips and lightweight wire are available in hardware stores. All other materials are jewelry supply items. (See the Demonstration on making a necklace, *Step 1*, at the end of the chapter.)

Egyptian Collar Necklace With Earrings

Make a cardboard pattern to use as a cutting mold for the necklace pendants. The pattern for the illustrated necklace measures 1" across the top and widens to 1¼" at the bottom. Each disk is 2" long.

Roll out a uniform slab of clay and cut out enough disks to form the necklace, plus two for the earrings. Be sure to dip your cutting knife into water after each slice.

Preparing the Pieces for Stringing

Use a pointed tool to make your holes for the stringing wire. Since this is a heavy necklace which will fit around the neck, you should make two rows of holes for extra strength and for better fit. The first hole should be made about ¼" from the top, the second hole ½" from the top. Pierce through from side to side. (See the Demonstration on making a necklace, *Step 2*, at the end of the chapter.)

Lay the pieces next to each other and check the alignment of the holes. Let them lie flat while drying.

The holes for hanging the earrings are pierced from front to back and, of course, just one in each earring is sufficient. (See the Demonstration on making a necklace, *Step 3*, at the end of the chapter.) When the earrings are dry, put the jump ring through the hole and attach an earring wire to the jump ring. The reason you will attach your earring findings before you varnish is that the earrings dangle and reveal two sides. You will want to design *both* sides. By having them all ready to hang, you can varnish both sides at once. The pieces for the necklace should be handled individually and not strung together until all are complete. (See the Demonstration on making a necklace, *Step 4*, at the end of the chapter.)

When the clay is hardened, sand it smooth and paint with any type of background paint or stain.

Designing the Necklace and Earrings

There should be a uniformity of mood and color in the design of these pieces. It is best to plan the design so that each pendant is complete in itself; in this way, there will be no "break" in the design as the necklace moves during wear. While each pendant is complete, there should be a total pattern, a story, when all the pieces are lined up. The two illustrated necklaces both accomplish this design plan.

One necklace is stained a wood color and tells an over-all story of romance through ladies and gentlemen facing each other on adjoining pendant beads. The earrings carry out the same theme, a gentleman on one side, a lady on the other. An interplay of reds and blues helps to carry through the note of unity.

Figure 92. *An Egyptian collar necklace stained mahogany and designed with figures from* Ladies' Amusement *carries out a romantic theme. The pinks and blues look well against the wood tones.*

Figure 93. *Here are earrings to match the wood-stained necklace.*

Figure 94. *Another Egyptian collar necklace, painted a dramatic black with designs from the* Crystal Palace Exhibition Catalogue, *is done in hot pinks, oranges, yellows, with green accents.*

Figure 95. *These earrings match the necklace in Figure 94.*

Another necklace decorated with illustrations from a facsimile catalog of *The Crystal Palace Exhibition of 1851* has a theme which emanates from the center bead which shows a tiny palace. Lions, griffons, ladies in waiting, angels, and statues surround each side of the palace making a regal scene. Again, each bead stands as an independent unity. The flying cherubs of one bead are repeated on the earrings; they carry through the theme, and underscore the airiness of the dangling ear drops. (See Figures 92, 93, and 94).

Finishing Ceramic Decoupage Jewelry

Either varnish or lacquer-based finishes are acceptable. This is a good time to try the lacquer-type finishes since jewelry seems to call for a fast finish. No matter what your finish, though, sand, steel wool, and wax with care.

Repairing Ceramic Decoupage Jewelry

One of the drawbacks of ceramic jewelry is that it *is* breakable; something can drop and chip. If you have ever discussed this with ceramists you will think all is lost. After all, you cannot add wet clay to dry clay without expecting cracks. What to do? The answer is bread dough.

This marvelous material has already been used for stuffed and molded decoupage designs and to make attractive little flowers (Chapter 6). Now, get out a slice of white bread, some white glue, and glycerine (one slice without crusts, ¾ teaspoon glue, ¼ teaspoon glycerine), knead it all together, and see how it works as a sturdy and smooth repairer. It blends so well with a ceramic finish that only the most astute eye will spot the "fix."

How to Repair a Nick

Suppose you have a nick at the corner of an earring or a pendant. All you have to do is break off a small bit of the kneaded dough to fill the nick, remove the dough and coat it with glue. Then, press the dough, glue side down, into the chip. Remove any dough which oozes out with a toothpick. Then, allow to harden overnight. The next day you can touch up with paint and apply one or two coats of decoupage finish.

Save the leftover bread dough in wax paper in the refrigerator. I will describe more uses for it in Chapter 12.

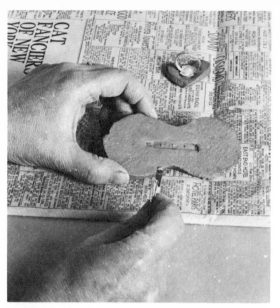

Making a Pin. *Use your jewelry finding to make an indentation into the wet clay. This makes cementing easier when the clay is hard. In this illustration a pinback is being indented into the back of a pin. A ring and ring base are at hand for the same procedure.*

Making a Barrette. *The clay barrette over a hump mold balloon. When the clay is leather hard it may be pulled away from the mold, which will have given it just the right contour to comfortably fit the human head.*

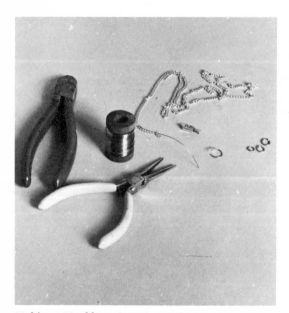

Making a Necklace. *Step 1. All the jewelry supplies needed to make the necklace. You can see the type of earring wires used for the drop earrings by looking at the finished illustrations.*

Making a Necklace. *Step 2. A toothpick dipped in water is used to put holes through from side to side for the necklace.*

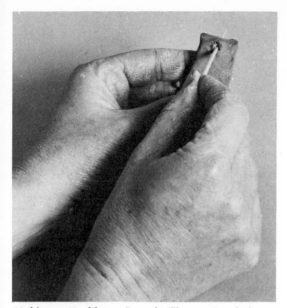

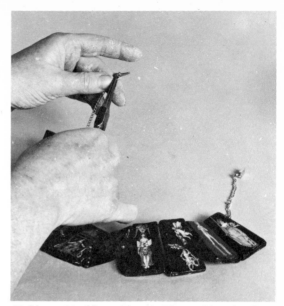

Making a Necklace. Step 3. The earring holes go from front to back.

Making a Necklace. Step 4. The necklace has been designed, varnished, and rubbed. Two wires have been strung through the two rows of holes. These wires have been tied together. A jump ring was used to connect the stringing wire with a piece of necklace chain. A box clasp is now being attached for closing.

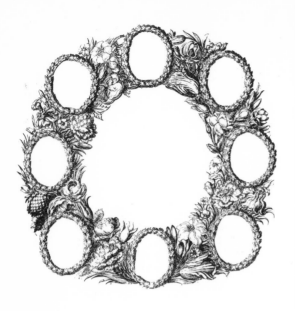

Figure 96. Here is an example of using a decoupage print to tell a story with photographs. The large center could hold a photo of a baby, with the little scrolls containing snapshots of the baby's growth. The same print could also be used to tell the progressive story of a marriage. The combination of the Baroque prints with very modern photograph materials lends itself very well to this type of decoupage.

Figure 97. A slim standing rock serves as an album for our family's winter sports activities. This side is devoted to skiing; the other side has skating scenes. The enclosing scrolls are a soft green with red ribbons. Two garlands of flowers draw a connecting line between front and back. The daisies were too slim for pictures so they are decorated with father's and mother's names on one side, brother's and sister's names on the other.

Figure 98. A pin combines black and white photographs with brilliantly colored flowers.

Figure 99. A trinket box is covered with mother-of-pearl, a family portrait, and garlands of flowers.

10

PHOTO DECOUPAGE AND OTHER MODERN MATERIALS

Let us consider your family snapshot as part of a decoupage composition. This can be an amusing and very personal piece of art for your home or a gift anyone would treasure.

Now, please do not rush out and grab a snapshot to mount on a piece of wood and cover with varnish. A frame or a photo lamination available from any photo shop can do this and probably do it better. What I have in mind is a very sparing use of photo materials combined with hand-colored flowers, borders, ribbons, and scrolls. By carefully combining a variety of photographic materials with interesting decoupage print materials and planning the design as part of an interesting background, you will be using your snapshot to make a personalized statement which transcends the ordinary framed photograph and becomes a piece of art; it is a bit sentimental perhaps, but that is what family albums are all about.

If you find a large scroll and combine it with lots of small scrolls you have an opportunity to have a miniature photograph album on one large plaque (Figure 96). A large photograph of a newly-wed couple might serve as a central focus and little pictures all around could tell the story of the marriage. They could progress from honeymoon to first home, first baby, anniversaries, etc. Or, the central focus could be a newborn baby, with progressive pictures of the baby's growth.

Photograph decoupage can be mounted on boxes, plaques, pins, ceramic disks (greenware or handmade), and stones to hang, wear, or stand up (Figures 97, 98, 99, 100, and 101).

Since photographs are usually printed on heavy paper, they should be peeled or you will find yourself needing forty or more coats of finish to sink in your design. Colored photographs disintegrate when wet and must be used dry, or without thinning.

Making a Photo-Decoupage Picture

Let us examine the charming picture of two children playing with a hand-colored yellow bird and circled with a wreath of hand-colored roses and discover how it was made (Figure 102).

First, two pictures were combined into one. They were two of my favorite snapshots. Because both children were involved with the same activity, and the snapshots were taken at a time when the brother and sister subjects still adored each other, I wanted to combine the two snapshots into one really memorable picture. My main interest was in capturing the children's expression of pure joy, so I eliminated all the extraneous background material. This included the balloons and yet when combining the pictures, I did have to plan for some sort of focal design to replace the balloons. The hand-colored bird, which I found more interesting and attractive than the balloons, provided the perfect solution. The roses seemed a just right sort of border for this idyllic little scene. (See the Demonstration on photo decoupage, *Step 1*, at the end of the chapter.)

Not all photograph designs need involve a combination of pictures. However, to make a photograph into an original piece of decoupage, rather than a repasted picture, you should do as much redesigning and add as much decoupage material as possible.

Preparing the Photo

The photos were soaked in cool water for half a minute, dried off, and placed face down on a clean surface. By scratching gently at the corner with a fingernail, the backing lifted and peeled off quite easily. (See the Demonstration on photo decoupage, *Step 2*, at the end of the chapter.)

109

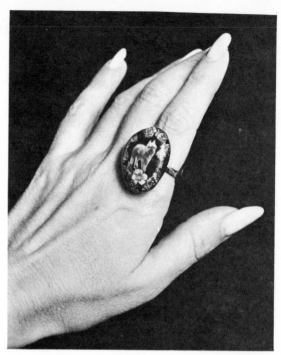

Figure 100. A humorous contrast is presented: a modern girl in jeans, holding a twentieth-century dog, enclosed by a baroque cartouche. The background is black, the cartouche bright orange and yellow.

Figure 101. A stone ring, painted black, immortalizes a favorite pet.

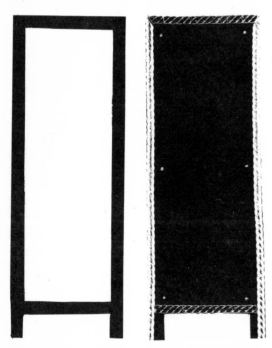

Figure 102. (Left) The frame for a handmade screen. (Right) The same frame with the Masonite panels nailed in place and a decorative trim attached around the edges of the panel.

Figure 103. The completed photo decoupage and frame is shown here from our step-by-step demonstration.

Figure 104. Here is a box designed with pictures from a collector's item book, reproduced with a photocopy machine, and colored by hand. It took sixty coats of varnish to sink the designs.

Photographs peel so easily that it is important not to peel them too thin or else you will have a wrinkly, hard-to-handle film rather than a thin layer of paper and photograph.

The peeled picture should be allowed to dry thoroughly before cutting. Cut as carefully as you would a decoupage print, but do not expect to be able to do the sort of fine feathery cutting that you can do with prints. Cutting photographs is limited in terms of creative technique, so use the photograph material sparingly. When pasting down, it is best to paste the photograph materials first, and then the decoupage prints.

Finishing

When finishing your photo decoupage, do not worry about the finish harming the photos. Neither lacquer-based finish nor varnish will harm a photograph surface. Since photographs are such modern material, you may prefer to work with a fast-building clear lacquer. Do not rush the sanding, though. You should apply a minimum of ten coats of lacquer finish or fifteen coats of varnish, before attempting to sand. When you do sand, do not use sandpaper stronger than No. 400, and finish with the No. 600. If you rub through the black and white photograph, there is no way to touch up. When the photo surface has been rubbed off, it is gone forever. You can use polymer gloss medium as your pasting and glazing agent. This requires no rubbing down and will give a textured finish.

You may wish to carry through the personal touch of photo decoupage with a handmade frame.

Making a Papier-Mâché Frame

To make a frame, first take your photo decoupage or a cardboard disk of the same size and center it against a piece of corrugated cardboard. Outline the disk, holding your pencil at an angle so that your outline will be somewhat larger than the actual disk. This is to allow for easy fit when you cement your disk with the design later on.

Mix some instant papier-mâché and apply this everywhere except the outlined center part. The mash application should be ¼" thick. If you want a raised rim, you can model this with your fingers. You can make any sort of indented pattern with bottle caps, serrated knives, or orange sticks. (See the Demonstration on the papier-mâché frame, *Steps 1 and 2*, at the end of the chapter.)

Bead Trim

To make a bead trim such as the one in the illustrated frame press your beads into the soft mash texture. Press the beads hard enough to make a deep impression and remove them. The beads will be glued into these recesses later, when the mâché has hardened. To make a stand-up easel, cut a piece of strong cardboard as shown (Figure 102). Glue this on at the folded top part and push out the legs. (See the Demonstration on the papier-mâché frame, *Steps 3 and 4*, at the end of the chapter.)

When the frame is dry, apply two coats of acrylic gesso to both sides of the frame. (See the Demonstration on making the papier-mâché frame, *Step 5*, at the end of the chapter.)

Finishing the Frame

You may use any kind of paint to finish your frame. The illustrated frame has an antique gold finish. The frame was painted with gold paint and when this was dry, some black water-based paint was diluted with water and applied over the gold. Since the paint was thinned, it did not fully cover the gold which shimmered through the black. A paper towel was used to rub off excess black paint. This type of antique effect can be achieved by combining other colors. Usually you can use something very bright as your main color and then wash it down with a diluted darker shade. For example, burnt orange washed over yellow, dark blue over light blue, umber over gold.

Instead of using beads, you could also embed string into the wet instant mâché. This would not have to be removed, but could be allowed to dry right into the mâché mixture.

You could varnish your photo decoupage in or out of the frame. I would suggest out. The frame should have two coats of decoupage finish, front and back. No rubbing is needed.

Photocopying Machines and Decoupage

The subject of photographs naturally brings to mind the question of reproducing materials from books with the photocopying machines now in most libraries and many drugstores. One would

---

Plate 1. (Right) A music-papered plaque.

112

Plate 2. (Above) A well-designed
lunchbox bag lives a second
life as a flower holder.

Plate 3. (Right) A footed box.
Yesterday a junk store item,
today an objet d'art.

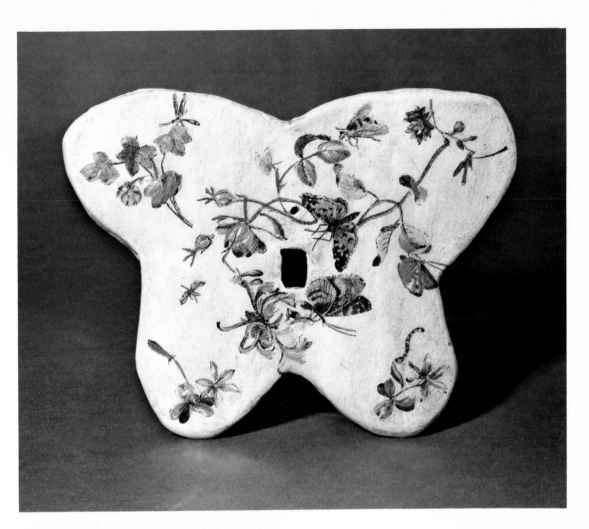

Plate 4. (Above) A handmade ceramic switchplate.

Plate 5. (Left) This stone's interesting slant offered a real design challenge.

Plate 6. (Above) *A complete description of how this screen was designed and built can be found in Chapter 13.*

Plate 7. (Right) *A closeup of two scenes from the screen.*

116

Plate 8. (Above) A painted metal tin designed with Godey figures and flowers.

Plate 9. (Above right) The third dimension is achieved with the raised level and paper-sculpture techniques.

Plate 10. (Right) A humidor decorated with hand-and ready-colored prints.

Plate 11. (Left) One side of a two-way slate pendant.

Plate 12. (Below) A box hand-built to fit its romantic, decorative theme.

Plate 13. An elegant box with a coordinated decoupage design extending to its fold-out drawers.

Plate 14. Shape, color, and design work beautifully in this completely handmade decoupage.

Plate 15. *(Right) Ceramic repoussé gives an added dimension to this mosaic owl vase.*

Plate 16. *(Center) A well-sized bisque egg box is decorated on the top, bottom, and inside.*

Plate 17. *(Bottom) Black and white prints against yellow provide a stunning effect without the need to hand color.*

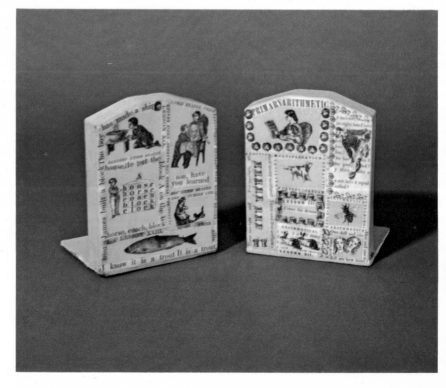

imagine that this would be an interesting and easy way to reproduce pictures inexpensively.

These machines are being improved all the time. However, at present, most of them reproduce on paper so thick and hard in texture that it takes many, many coats of varnish to sink this paper in. Also, the paper resists being thinned with a razor or being sponged off in layers.

Another drawback is that the reproduction is a muddy sort of gray with a filmy coating which is extremely hard to color. It can be done, but the job is harder and the colors are not as deep as most people would desire. Some of the big office machines have already overcome these difficulties, but most of us do not have access to them.

Once I did use this reproduction method in spite of difficulties. I had a Kate Greenaway book which was a collector's item and I wanted to make a design on a recipe box and have the book and box as a unit (Figure 104). Also, I needed to reduce the size of the pictures that I wanted to reproduce and this was only possible with the library photocopy machine. (Note, however, that not all machines available have the regular and legal-size paper adjustments). The result was most satisfying, but a word of warning: it took *sixty* coats of varnish to sink in the designs.

An inexpensive printing process, available in most towns and cities, will be described in detail in Chapter 13.

Newspapers and Magazines for Decoupage

Those who are attracted to modern and timely designs will invariably ask about using prints from the Sunday supplement magazines, current magazines, and newspapers. For fine antique varnished and hand-rubbed decoupage, these materials are usually not worthwhile.

The gloss of most black and white magazine illustrations resists coloring and the verso (backside) printing tends to show through under varnish. Colored illustrations might bleed. There are, of course, all types of magazines and some publications print on fine-paper stock which can be used for decoupage. In many instances these modern materials lend themselves to photocollage and montage. They are cousins of decoupage, but not the same. Photocollage involves overlapping designs; montage involves mounting whole sheets onto surfaces; neither one depends upon finish, but *strictly design*. Decoupage consists of exact cutting, designing, *and* a fine finish.

Since the category of magazine publications involves such a wide range of papers and inks, you must test anything you want to use as it comes along and then make your decision. Spray both the front and the back to see if the colors hold and how much of the verso will show through when wet. If the inks bleed, do not use it. If the verso shows through but the material is very unusual you might decide to live with the faults of the material. If you cannot color the material, you could design in black and white, with bright backgrounds or colored accessory designs.

Sometimes, while magazine materials cannot be used physically, they can serve as inspiration in working with more usable materials. For example, a series of very modern ads from a sportswear shop inspired a layout for a box bag which consisted of costumes from old Godey books and related prints (Figure 105).

As for newspapers, these are definitely out in terms of decoupage. Newspapers are printed on the cheapest type of paper. They defy coloring and get weak and blurry under varnish. However, you *can* use decoupage cutting and designing when you finish off mâché objects with a top layer of cut newspaper materials.

Newspaper Finishes

While you can finish off a papier-mâché object with decoupage cutting and designing techniques, you cannot expect the same finish and feel of genuine decoupage. When we discussed papier-mâché in Chapter 5, it was in terms of creating a handmade, sturdy, and smooth background for traditional decoupage designing. The boxes and plaques were made out of smoothly layered newspaper and cardboard. The bases were painted and treated like wooden and metal items. The designs were varnished, sanded, and waxed. However, if you like really modern methods of design you might make a papier-mâché base and when you have applied enough layers of torn rather than evenly layered strips to give you a strong base, you would simply add a top decorative layer of newspaper. The top layer, instead of being put on with casually torn crisscross strips of newspaper, is carefully cut and pasted down in the decoupage manner. Four or five coats of decoupage lacquer finish can be applied, more as a protective coating than to achieve any special patina. Sometimes a project or idea lends itself to this type of treatment. For example, a large egg made with layers of torn

Figure 105. A modern newspaper ad inspired a design executed with prints from old Godey's Books, *a book on porcelain, and gold paper braid. The box is wood stained, the designs colored with a complete palette.*

newspaper strips over a balloon mold. The two top layers of the egg were done in the decoupage manner. First, a checkered background was taken from a Volkswagen ad; second, eyes were cut out of a newspaper cosmetic ad and arranged to form a border and daisy design. The egg could have been cut apart, given a box lip and rim and used as a very modern desk accessory (Figure 106).

The Most Usable Modern Materials

Catalogs can run the gamut from strictly throwaway stuff to good usable materials. Flower, book, and travel catalogs are often very good. Be as selective in the materials you choose as you would be in selecting things during your more conventional catalog browsing.

Gift wraps, stationery, and bridge pads are often filled with attractive designs, especially for those who like to use ready-colored materials (Figure 107). When using anything printed in color, it is always a good idea to find out if the colors will bleed. First, spray and test-varnish a small portion.

As already discussed in Chapter 1, publishers are making available facsimile editions of marvelous black and white engraved materials. These editions are wonderful for the decoupeur. Also, many children's books are inexpensive and publishers keep editions of favorite illustrators such as Tasha Tudor and Kate Greenaway in print at all times. Library book sales and second-hand book sales are good sources for materials.

Often these materials can be combined to create very interesting designs (Figure 108).

Figure 106. Here is an example of papier-mâché base and finish. The top layers are cut and designed in the decoupage manner, but the over-all is really more papier-mâché than decoupage.

Figure 107. Gift-wrap flowers were used to give new life to an old set of porch furniture.

Figure 108. *Old prints and modern gift wraps can be ingeniously combined—as with this mirror framed with proscenium and orchestra, curtains and balcony—from old French toy prints and gift-wrap paper. The drama begins when you look in the mirror!*

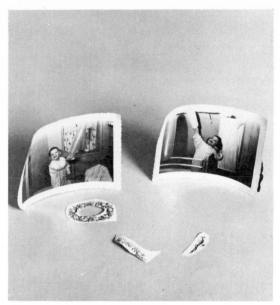

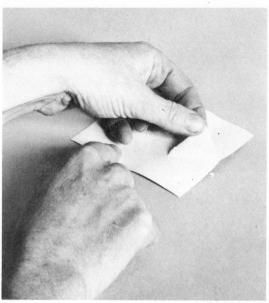

Preparing for Photo Decoupage. Step 1. Here are two photos which will be combined with hand-colored decoupage designs.

Preparing for Photo Decoupage. Step 2. To peel a photo, dip it in cool water, then lay it face down. Dry off the back and get hold of a corner with your fingernail. The paper will peel off.

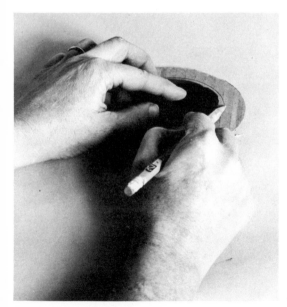

Making a Papier-Mâché Frame. Step 1. The disk with the decoupage design is outlined against corrugated cardboard which will serve as a frame. The outline should be drawn at an angle so that it is larger than the disk for easy fit later on.

Making a Papier-Mâché Frame. Step 2. Instant papier-mâché has been mixed with water and is attached all around the border portion of the frame. Glue should be applied to the cardboard before the papier-mâché mixture is placed down.

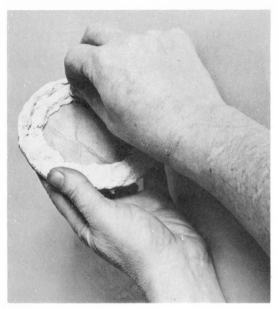

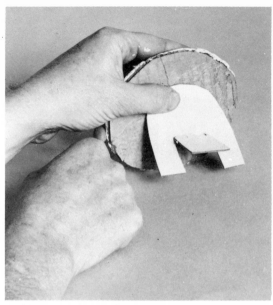

Making a Papier-Mâché Frame. Step 3. Beads which will be cemented in later are indented while the papier-mâché is wet.

Making a Papier-Mâché Frame. Step 4. A stand-up easel, also made out of cardboard, is glued to the back of the frame.

Making a Papier-Mâché Frame. Step 5. When the frame is hard, two coats of gesso are applied to the front, back, and stand.

11

DECOUPAGE WITHOUT RUBBING

Your varnishing and rubbing process will protect your finished decoupage pieces so that they can last long enough to become heirlooms. However, there are times when you want to apply your coloring, cutting, and designing skills to surfaces which will be subject to extreme heat, knocking about, rinsing. There are various forms of decoupage which eliminate varnishing altogether.

Decoupage Under Glass

This is good for table tops, ashtrays, plates, canisters, and, if you really get ambitious, lamps. The chief difference from traditional varnished and rubbed decoupage is that your cutouts are placed *under* rather than on top of a surface, so that the glass replaces the varnish and other finishing processes. Your glue is put on top of the cutouts and the cutouts are then glued to the underside of glass. Paint is used in back of the cutouts. The result is most attractive and intriguing. It is always fun to watch someone unfamiliar with this technique try to figure out how you got the designs between the glass and the painted background.

Making a Glass Canister

A canister available in most dime stores is a popular under-glass project. I will describe how you would glue your cutouts and paint up against them.

You can use ready- or hand-colored prints. I feel hand coloring gives more interest to this type of project. Since no varnish will cover the colored portions you should not seal the prints. They will adhere better without the plastic coating.

The next step is one which usually confuses people trying this for the first time. The glue is put *on top of the design*. Invariably someone forgets

and puts it on the underside and then has to wait for this glue to dry. Apply the glue sparingly, but be sure everything is covered. (See the Demonstration on the glass canister, *Step 1*, at the end of the chapter.)

Take your design and press the glue-coated design side up against the inside of the canister. (See the Demonstration on the glass canister, *Step 2*, at the end of the chapter.)

When your design is exactly where you want it, press up against the underside with a damp, almost dry, sponge. You are pressing to get out all the glue that is still between the top of the print and the glass. If you look closely you will see the glue actually moving. If you have applied your glue sparingly, there should be a minimum of glue to squeeze out.

When you have pressed carefully with your barely damp sponge, using your fingers to press up against the sponge, get out a pressing tool and press down with that. (See the Demonstration on the glass canister, *Step 3*, at the end of the chapter.) Remove the sponge and test your designs with your fingernails to be sure everything is down tight. It is vitally important that you have no loose edges or, when you start to paint, the paint is going to run under those loose edges and ruin your design.

Drying and Finishing

Let your design dry, *really* dry. Overnight is preferable. People who are impatient use hair driers to blow on the design. This is okay. The main thing is to let those designs and the glue dry thoroughly. Be sure everything is down tight, and will stay tight.

When you are satisfied that everything is dry and tight, clean up any glue and finger smudges

Figure 110. An oriental motif is placed under the glass of an interestingly shaped ashtray.

Figure 109. Glass canisters are not expensive in dime stores. This one is painted a bright gold. The prints of old English street vendors are in browns and blue-grays. A canister like this would be attractive in a kitchen or in a bathroom to hold cotton balls. If the designs were placed on the outside and covered with varnish, then using the canister in a bathroom with a steamy shower would not be recommended.

Figure 111. This looks like a delft plate. The designs were done completely in the almost purplish blue which identifies delftware. White acrylic gesso was used as a background paint.

with a corner of a sponge or a cotton swab. If you leave dirt, you will be painting it in later. I have found that after I sponge clean and dry the plate with a lint-free cloth, a good final tool for getting my glass spotless is tissue eyeglass cleaners. Use these to polish up all the glass spots not covered by designs.

While you did not have to seal the top of your prints, you must seal the back surface before you paint. This is to prevent paint from slipping under edges. I find the easiest and most effective way to do this is to apply two to four coats of clear plastic spray. Be sure you spray lightly. If you soak your print, it will be likely to come loose. Also, if you apply too heavy a spray coating, bubbly marks will form against the glass. The idea is to apply a mist of spray from an arm's length distance. Let this dry thoroughly. Apply another coat, then a third, and perhaps even a fourth.

You are now ready to paint. Any paint is suitable though I find water-based paints seem to adhere best to glass. Since I like the look of milk glass, I often use white gesso as my paint. This adheres very well. The illustrated canister (Figure 109) is painted with yellow oil paint. So you see, there are absolutely no hard and fast rules.

Apply the paint lightly. You can pat rather than stroke it on. Start in the middle of the canister, work towards the bottom and then out towards the edges. Your first coat will probably look rather streaky and will not cover completely. A second coat should do the trick.

After your second coat of paint is dry, apply one or two coats of varnish for a smoothly sealed back. Your project is now complete.

Fun Projects With Polymer Gloss

The best way to handle a just for fun project is to use a commonly available artist's medium known as polymer gloss. This will double as a pasting-down *and* glazing agent. It is water soluble and requires no sanding or rubbing. It gives a tough, durable, textured finish. The look is more like that of an oil painting. While this is an attractive finish and can be appreciated in its own right, it should not be compared to traditional decoupage. In using polymer, you will be using decoupage cutting, coloring, and designing skills.

I would like to stress that while you may skip the long-term crafts techniques of varnishing and sanding, good design should not be sacrificed. Give your design plan the time and thought which any

Figure 112. A fun project is clogs with gaily colored flowers and butterflies.

Figure 113. Another good polymer-medium project is a giant key holder. Since keys may scratch the holder, the polymer-textured finish is a necessary protection.

Figure 114. A lunchbox bag designed to withstand the tides of fashion. It is decorated with hand-colored designs from old magazines, against an antique white ground. It has been retired as a bag, but makes a handsome holder for bread dough roses and other artificial flowers. (See Color Plate 2.)

Figure 115. Another lunchbox bag glazed with polymer medium and done with decoupage designs to hold interest beyond the fad stage of the bag. The background is an orange-yellow. The designs are taken from gift wraps and catalogs and very carefully applied to maintain good gaze motion within a rather busy surface.

Figure 116. A folded paper design cut free form by a Polish folk artist. The base color is black, but there are additional overlay cuts in pink and yellow.

creative work requires. Any place, be it a serious *objet d'art* or a whim of the season, deserves your respect. Otherwise, you might as well buy what you want ready made and forget about handcrafting altogether.

Subjects for Polymer Finish

Eyeglass cases, diaries, telephones, and albums are usually made of materials associated with short-term rather than long-term use and are therefore not suitable for varnished and rubbed decoupage. However, they can be gay conversation pieces when decorated with interesting designs and finished with polymer medium.

A design from a wallpaper, translated to a plain window shade, and inexpensive box, or a tray table and then glazed with polymer medium can add an attractive decorative touch to a room. Wallpaper is much too pulpy and thick for decoupage, but the polymer medium offers the opportunity to work with these types of designs.

Shoes will eventually and inevitably wear out, but what pleasure and fun it has been to wear my flower-sprigged clogs! (See Figure 112.)

Lunchbox Handbags

Handbags made out of workmen's lunchpails seemed destined to be a passing fad from their first and immediately popular appearance upon the fashion accessory scene. People who never heard the word decoupage suddenly snipped whiskey bottle labels and magazine illustrations, paying little attention to cutting or proper coordination of designs, backgrounds, and color. These would-be decoupeurs used hard shellacs for a finish. This soon chipped so that even if the fashion had not faded, the bags would have been too physically beat up for further use.

Lunchbox bags decorated with true decoupage cutting and designing skills were able to survive this fad. They lent themselves to nostalgic designs since the lunchpail itself, like old Coke bottles and beer trays, might one day become a part of the memorabilia scene. My designs for some of these bags were carefully chosen to illustrate a bygone era and they go with the base, which might one day fit into the same category. The designs were hand colored. The box was painted to remove the harshness of the raw metal. Acrylic medium was used to paste down the designs and to glaze them. The bag was never nicked; the designs were perfectly protected. Today, while no longer in use as a handbag, it serves as a most attractive home accessory, an artificial flower holder (Figure 114). When my daughter was working on a similar project, she also chose her designs carefully. She was less conscious of the potential of her bag, but she did choose a theme which to her presented a timeless interest: pets. This bag, while no longer a high fashion accessory, still adds a useful and attractive note to her desk as a container for crayons and pencils and other desk-top miscellany (Figure 115).

A Composition Board Album

A composition board album gains durability with polymer medium, and artistic charm with decoupage. The design surface of these types of albums is pebbly and thus not inherently right for varnishing and sanding. This pebbly surface does blend very well with the texture of polymer medium. The illustrated album was painted with one coat of white acrylic gesso and one coat of white water-based paint. I will describe how the polymer finish was done, step-by-step.

First, apply a coat of polymer gloss medium to your background and allow to dry. The medium goes on white and dries clear. Do not worry about marks, this is part of the medium's makeup. (See the Demonstration on an album, *Step 1*, at the end of the chapter.)

When the first coat of polymer is dry (about ten minutes) apply a second coat, and immediately place your designs in the wet surface. Press them down and be sure to remove any air bubbles. Whether you use white glue or gloss medium, and whether you varnish or not, anything that is pasted down must always be smoothed to avoid wrinkles and air bubbles. Use your roller, your fingers, or the back of a spoon, to press the designs down tight. (See the Demonstration on an album, *Step 2*, at the end of the chapter.)

When the second coat of polymer—with your designs embedded in it—is dry, apply a third coat *on top* of the design. The design will not disappear. The white film will again dry clear. Use your brush in an uneven, free way. Since you will have a textured surface anyway, you might as well make this texture look more interesting. Follow this third coat with two or three additional coats, always allowing the polymer to dry before applying a new coat. These last coatings are for protection and durability. (See the Demonstration on an album, *Step 3*, at the end of the chapter.)

Free-Form and Silhouette Cutting

Another type of decoupage which fits into this chapter of quick-finish techniques is inspired by the peasant art long practiced in Poland, Switzerland, China, Japan, and the Scandinavian countries. The peasant artists' designs range from tiny pictures to full-scale murals. Folk artists always cut their designs free form, from a single sheet of paper. If the cuts are made on folded paper, the final unfolded design will be doubled, achieving perfect symmetry (Figure 116). If the paper is pleated several times, accordion fashion, the picture can be extended, much like the chains of paper dolls which youngsters love to create. Any type of colored paper is effective and additional shapes of contrasting colored paper can be added. Black paper alone is very dramatic for achieving a silhouette effect. The free form of cutting is a good way to introduce youngsters to decoupage.

Using Decoupage for Silhouette Cutting

Those of you who feel the free-form style of cutting presents the same hurdle that drawing and painting did can use a decoupage design as a cutting guide. It will be fun to look at pictures in terms of choosing those which would lend themselves to silhouetting. You will find that figures are particularly suitable.

First, try a simple singlefold silhouette. Fold your paper in half, from left to right. The width of the folded paper should be the width of the widest part of your design. Each side of the design must touch at one point since this is the connection that keeps it all attached when opened up. Hold your design firmly in place, and cut with your best cutting technique. Now open up your paper and see how your figure has become a pair.

To obtain a whole row of designs, fold the paper several times, accordion fashion.

Since these types of cutouts will have none of the shading of the guideline pictures, there are no shadings and highlights to bring out under varnish. Instead, place your designs under glass or put them on a plaque and coat with a few coats of acrylic gloss medium.

Decorating a Glass Canister. Step 1. Glue is put on top of the cutout. Apply the glue sparingly, but be sure everything is covered.

Decorating a Glass Canister. Step 2. The cutout is pressed up against the underside of the glass with a damp sponge or cloth.

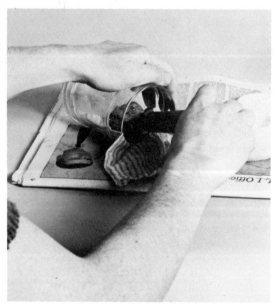

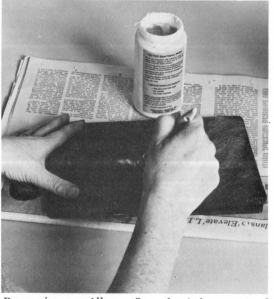

Decorating a Glass Canister. Step 3. A roller is used to further press out the glue. A damp cloth or sponge will also pick up the glue on the rest of the glass.

Decorating an Album. Step 1. A base coat of polymer gloss medium is applied to prime the background.

Decorating an Album. Step 2. *A second coat of polymer is applied when the first dries and the design is placed into the wet medium. Then it is smoothed out with a roller. The wax paper is used to protect the design surface.*

Decorating an Album. Step 3. *When the previous coat has dried, additional coats of protective polymer glaze are applied on top of the designs. Always wait for drying between applications.*

Figure 117. Three little dancers (upper left) become a whole stage of dancers when cut against accordion folds of black paper (center left). One portion of the figure must touch each edge to maintain the connection, in this case the braids of the little girl at right and the collar of the little boy at left (see the whole row of figures from 4 accordion folds in the center). A single figure placed against a single fold of paper (lower left) gains a partner in silhouette (lower right).

Figure 119. Up and down borders afford interesting design possibilities. In the original print the children were peering over a brick wall. They were separated and rearranged with a tailored up and down border and a flower border across a rim.

Figure 118. The figures in this egg fitted the upper part of the box. To unify the design, a ledge of daisies was placed around the top of the rim. A sprig of daisies is repeated at the tip.

12

EGGS-QUISITE DECOUPAGE

Throughout the ages, artists have been fascinated with the egg as a symbol of the life force in such works as the dome of St. Peter's Basilica, Brancusi's "Newborn," Dali's surrealistic creations. Men of wit and wisdom are characterized and caricatured as "eggheads."

As for egg decoration, to many people Easter would not be Easter without eggs to decorate, whether in the simple and colorful tradition of the folk artist, or in the more ornate manner originated by the artist Fabergé. The Imperial Eggs which Fabergé created for the Russian Tsarist family became world renowned.

Egg decoration has become a year-round craft for many artists. Decoupeurs are no exception. To quote Oscar Wilde: "An egg is always an adventure! It may be different."

Indeed, nothing need remain the same except the basic shape. Borders, background colors, and the placement of designs can be varied in an infinite number of ways. The eggs themselves may range from china nesting eggs to large egg boxes. They may be bought or hand fashioned.

Even the stands on which eggs sit or from which they hang are a source of creative inspiration. With a little ingenuity you can use inexpensive castoffs or electrical supply items to make these stands or you can make more elaborate and elegant stands from wire and papier-mâché.

Because egg decoupage seems to incorporate so much of this book's whole concept about designing, craftsmanship, and making use of auxiliary crafts, there is a whole chapter to introduce you to a variety of "good eggs."

Wooden Egg Boxes

A decorated egg is pretty, but an egg which opens up to hold a pair of earrings, cufflinks, paper clips, or other tiny things is a special decorative treat. These eggs come in unfinished basswood (see Suppliers List), and screw apart. They sit on the wide bottom. Working around the opening and towards the graduated top offers lots of design challenge.

Designing Wooden Eggs

If you are planning a design with figures, you have a choice of crossing the opening (in which case the figure will have to be sliced through with a razor blade after gluing) or, if your figures are shorter, you can provide them with a ledge which will also serve to hide the opening. (See Figures 117 and 118.) A series of panels to enclose individual designs sometimes works out. These panels may vary from hand-colored borders (Figure 119), to gold paper braids, to mother-of-pearl flakes (Figure 120).

I have seen dozens of decorated eggs but I have never seen the same design or colors. They are stunning in black with uncolored designs. The design motifs can be faces, flowers, modern or antique themes.

Wooden Eggstands

Unless you sand the bottoms of the wooden egg boxes very flat before you paint and design them (and I do not recommend this, since it will somewhat spoil the shape), you should provide them with a little stand so that they sit firmly. My own favorite is a ¾" lock nut available in any electrical supply store for a few cents. When sprayed or rubbed with gold, no one would ever guess this was not an expensive decorator stand. Bottlecaps covered with strips of gold paper braid can also be used as stands. A cardboard circle with a narrow cardboard rim can be made very sturdy and given a

Figure 120. *These regal Grecian figures seemed to call for something elegant in the way of separating panels, so mother-of-pearl flakes were used.*

Figure 121. *A message of peace is most appropriate for an Easter gift. Black and white cherubic letters are used for this sampler. The top part of the egg continues the message with the words "truth, beauty, and honor" in italic.*

Figure 122. *A well-sized ceramic bisque egg box is decorated on top, bottom, and inside. The figures are in greens, yellows, and blues. The borders are a Wedgwood blue. The background is white. (See Color Plate 16.)*

Figure 123. *A small bisque egg painted in silver with the designs in a brownish gold with accents of deep blue.*

nice texture with a covering of instant papier-mâché. While this mash mixture is wet you can indent a pattern with string, the side of a screw driver, or any similar instrument. When the mâché hardens it can be painted to match the wooden egg. (See the Demonstration on eggstands at the end of the chapter.) For a complete review of papier-mâché see Chapter 5.

Ceramic Bisque Eggs

Ceramic studios carry all sizes of greenware eggs. Large ones (Figure 122) make handsome candy dishes; small ones can be used as saccharine or jewelry holders (Figure 123). These eggs sit sideways and thus present an entirely new design viewpoint of the egg shape. Also, they have flat plate-like bottoms and require no stand.

If you have a ceramic studio near you, you will be buying these eggs in their soft or greenware state. The studio owner will show you how to clean up the greenware and then fire it to a bisque hard stage. Your eggs will look nice and white and the temptation might be to design right on top of this without painting. Beware! This white is a temporary finish. Your ceramic bisque egg must be painted. Oil paints should be sealed with clear spray or other sealer. Water-based paints can go directly onto the bisque. If the bisque is not 100% smooth, you can sand it with No. 400 sandpaper, used dry, before painting.

Ceramic studios carry nonfiring stains which can be used exactly like paint. Most of these stains are water based. They cover very well and come in a lovely assortment of shades. They cost no more than other paints and generally go much further.

Handmade Ceramic Eggs

When making your own egg shapes out of clay, you will want to review Chapter 8 on ceramic decoupage. You can work with self-hardening clay, or if you have access to a kiln, with firing clay. Just as we made pots over balloon molds (Figure 84), you can make eggs over balloon molds (Figure 124). I will review how this is done.

First, get some balloons which have long, rather than round, shapes. A small balloon is best. Then, roll out a large round slab of clay.

Use your own blown-up balloon as a guide to scratch a pattern of four sides of the balloon shape. The pattern will look like a four-petaled daisy. (See the Demonstration on making a bal-

Figure 124. A handmade ceramic egg was shaped over a balloon mold. The egg is just large enough to hold two American eagles.

Figure 125. A small ceramic egg was shaped by hand with its own little clay stand. A hole was left at the top to expedite handling during varnishing.

Figure 126. Small hand-shaped eggs can also be used as tree ornaments or as earrings. A hole is run from top to bottom for an attachment wire, which is knotted at the bottom of the egg.

Figure 127. China nesting eggs lend themselves to a touch of opulence. This one was painted a rich gold. The birds are colored blue.

loon-mold pot, *Steps 1 and 2*, at the end of Chapter 8.)

Cut out the petals, leaving the center intact. Now, weld the sides together around the balloon. While a pot may have a wide neck, the egg should close almost completely around the balloon, leaving an opening only large enough for the balloon to stick out.

When the clay is leather hard, deflate the balloon slowly and pull out of the small hole. This hole will be used as a connective with the stand.

To make the balloon stand, merely shape a sort of disk in your hand and attach a little coil to it. This coil or stick will fit up into the hole of the egg and hold it in place. (See the Demonstration on the clay eggstand at the end of the chapter.)

Very small eggs can be made by taking a ball of clay in your hand and shaping it until you have an egg that is satisfactory to you (Figure 125). Very small eggs made this way can be used as Christmas tree ornaments or earrings. In order to attach earring wires or tree hangers, poke a hole from top to bottom while the clay is wet and run a wire through the hole. Make a knot at the bottom so it cannot slip out (Figure 126).

China Nesting Eggs

At one time china nesting eggs were commonly found on every farm where they were used to encourage the hens to lay eggs. Today, they are becoming treasured antique store items. Unfortunately, as they became rarer and more popular, the prices have gone up. They can still be found in stores and at fairs. Anytime you find any of these china eggs for under a dollar, buy several.

The pure white china finish is best when left unpainted, though once in a while it is worth experimenting (Figure 127).

Nesting eggs are especially attractive when hung up. Before you start designing, you should attach something from which the egg can later be hung. By doing this, you solve the problem of how to hold the egg during varnishing. The best and most attractive hanger is a pronged bellcap which cements right over the egg tip. You can see a bellcap illustrated at the end of Chapter 4 in the demonstration on rocks and in Figures 42 and 128.

If you cannot find china eggs, try goose eggs which are available cleaned and blown. They are sturdy and very lovely. (See Suppliers List.) Regular kitchen eggs can be blown out and used for decoupage. However, today's eggs are rather thin-skinned and small, so they must be handled with care. The glue, decorations, and varnish *will* strengthen the eggs in the long run.

Styrofoam Eggs

Basically, styrofoam is totally unusable in terms of decoupage. It is much too rough textured and can never be made completely smooth. It would simply eat up varnish. Yet, it is possible to create a perfectly beautiful and smooth egg with decoupage designs and finish (Figure 29). How? The answer is bread dough!

This versatile ingredient seems to be cropping up over and over again. We used it to stuff prints in Chapter 6, to repair ceramic decoupage jewelry in Chapter 9, and to fill our handmade ceramic vases with bread dough flowers in Chapter 8. Now, here is bread dough again, this time as a covering for styrofoam which comes in so many interesting shapes and is extremely light.

How to Cover Styrofoam Eggs

We could cover our eggs with the same bread dough recipe used in earlier sections of this book. However, we will use a recipe which involves breadmaking ingredients rather than the bread itself. This is even smoother than the other formula and presents absolutely no shrinkage problem. It does require cooking.

Combine 2 cups of baking soda and 1 cup of cornstarch, 1-1/3 cups of water, and 2 teaspoons of glycerine. Cook this mixture over low heat, stirring constantly until the dough forms into a ball. Remove it from the pot, place on a wooden board, and pat down flat. When the dough cools, knead it as you would bread.

Unused dough should be stored in a tightly sealed plastic bag in the refrigerator.

Applying Bread Dough to a Styrofoam Egg

Press the dough into a thin sheet. Next, apply glue to the egg, and smooth pieces of the thin sheets of bread dough all around the egg. (See the Demonstration on the styrofoam egg, *Steps 1 and 2,* at the end of the chapter.) Keep smoothing with your hands until the entire egg is covered. Allow to dry overnight. If necessary, you can sand smoother with dry No. 400 sandpaper. Finally, design and varnish.

Figure 128. China nesting eggs can be left in their pure-white glass state. This one hangs from a handmade Fabergé type stand made with instant papier-mâché over a pipe cleaner armature.

Figure 129. A styrofoam egg was covered with bread dough to give it a smooth surface.

139

Papier-Mâché Stand for Eggs

Anything as special as these decoupage eggs deserves a special stand, a stand free and airy enough to permit the design to show. Once you learn to make the stand for the styrofoam egg, you will be able to make the stand from which the china nesting egg hangs (Figure 128).

Cut a corrugated cardboard circle for the bottom crossbar. Punch in three holes for legs. Make an armature out of pipe cleaners, pulling one end through each of the crossbar holes and knotting for ball-shaped feet. You could use ordinary wire but the pipe cleaners are easier to cover with papier-mâché. Cover the pipe cleaners with glue and work around the armature. (See the Demonstration on the papier-mâché stand at the end of the chapter.)

When the mâché has hardened, paint with two thin coats of gesso, then paint with the color of your choice. The illustrated stand was painted gold first, and then given an overlay of black paint thinned with water. The stand was trimmed with bread dough roses.

Making Bread Dough Roses

You will have bread dough left over from covering your styrofoam egg, or you could use the white bread, white glue, and glycerine recipe.

Take a very small ball of bread dough and shape it into a teardrop. This is the center of your rose. If you were to put this rose into a flower holder, you would attach a floral wire, its tip dipped in white glue, through this center petal. Next, make a number of little pea-shaped balls and shape them over your fingers, making the petals as thin as possible. Now, put a dab of white glue on the inside bottom of the petal and attach it to the center teardrop. Now, take your second petal and glue that around, overlapping as you go along. Use your fingers to curve the petal edges for a realistic look. (See the Demonstration on bread dough roses, *Steps 1, 2, and 3*, at the end of the chapter.)

Glue the finished rose to the stand while it is soft. When hardened, use a very thin brush to paint the rose. Protect it with two or three coats of varnish or lacquer.

The stand for the gold nesting egg (Figure 127) was also made of bread dough. Instead of rose petals, daisy leaves were cut and shaped around a center which was made by flattening a large pea-sized ball of dough into a base about the size of a bottle cap. (Instructions for forming daisy leaves may be found at the end of Chapter 6 in the Demonstration on making a bread dough daisy.) The pointy part of the egg was glued and pressed into the stand while the bread dough was still wet. The stand thus also served as something to hold onto during varnishing.

Eggstands. Here are some examples of eggstands for wooden egg boxes. From left to right: corrugated cardboard covered with papier-mâché, a bottle cap trimmed with gold paper braid, and a lock nut from an electrical supply store, rubbed with gold wax.

Making a Clay Eggstand. This stand can be made from a simple clay disk with a little dowel which will fit into the hole at the bottom of the egg. The little black knobs are attached for decoration to carry through the decorative design of the egg.

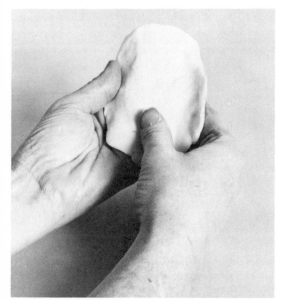

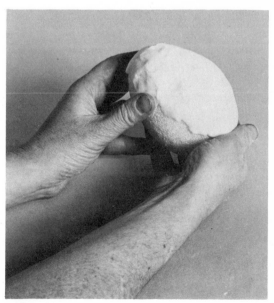

Making a Styrofoam Egg. Step 1. Bread dough is pressed into a thin layer.

Making a Styrofoam Egg. Step 2. The thin layer of bread dough is pressed around a styrofoam egg which has been covered with white glue.

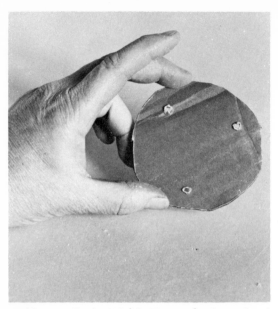

Making a Papier-Mâché Eggstand. Step 1. A corrugated cardboard circle will serve as a bottom crossbar for stand. Three holes are drilled through for the legs.

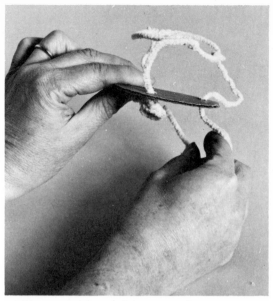

Making a Papier-Mâché Eggstand. Step 2. Pipe cleaners are tied together and pulled through the holes to form an armature.

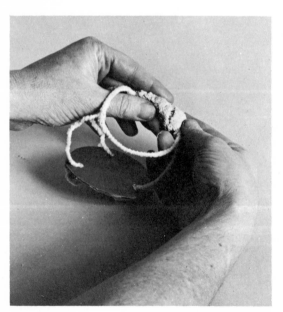

Making a Papier-Mâché Eggstand. Step 3. Instant papier-mâché is worked around the pipe cleaners, which have been covered with white glue.

Making Bread Dough Roses. Step 1. To make the center of the rose, form a tiny ball of bread dough into a teardrop. The rose for our stand will be without a stem, like the finished rose at the left. To use the rose in a holder, a flower wire should be attached to the rose center at the right.

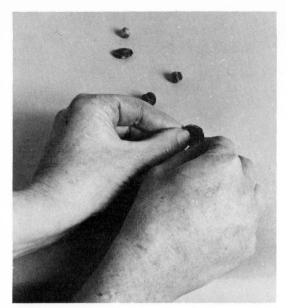 

Making Bread Dough Roses. Step 2. Tiny pea-sized balls are then rolled out for the rose petal. For each petal, the ball is pressed out and thinned with your thumb.

Making Bread Dough Roses. Step 3. A dab of glue is put at the bottom inside of the petal and it is then draped around the rose center. Leaves are added, one by one.

Figure 130. A screen was completely papered with pages from an early nineteenth-century treatise on antiquities. Prints of suns, hands, antiquities, and butterflies from various sources are superimposed.

13

SO YOU WANT TO MAKE
SOMETHING REALLY BIG!

Sooner or later your enthusiasm for decoupage will give rise to the urge to undertake at least one big project: a coffee table, a chest, a desk, a piano, a screen. If you have ever seen any of these big decoupaged pieces, this urge will become stronger and stronger; a large piece of decoupage is indeed magnificent.

A word of warning, though: be sure you really have the time, the patience, and the interest. Do not take on a big project before you have learned to handle some of the smaller ones described in this book. And do not expect to be done in the time it takes to put on the required number of varnish coats.

Your composition will take more planning; so will your search for materials. Forty coats of varnish are more likely to be needed than twenty coats. It is *not* advisable to save your rubbing until the very end. Instead, once you have completed twenty coats, you should rub and sand every seven coats until you are finished.

If you design only the front facing drawers of a chest, you should still paint or stain the entire piece you are doing. While you might not have to varnish continuously over the plain sides of your piece, you must be able to sand and rub the entire piece for a final uniform patina.

Discouraged? I hope not, for actually it *is* worth it. I am pointing out the pitfalls and drawbacks only to prevent you from starting something you *may* wish you had never begun.

Suggestions to Insure Success

The following suggestions are given not to discourage, but to insure that any attempt at a large piece will be successful and satisfying.

First, try your hand at decoupaging a fairly difficult box, one with drawers, doors, and hinges. This gives you experience in dealing with a number of design surfaces on one object.

Second, get your feet wet in terms of furniture design by tackling some miniature chests. Browse through toy stores and catalogs of manufacturers who supply doll collectors (see Suppliers List). There are many miniature screens, Venetian-type secretaries, and all sorts of intricate pieces. As you plan designs for these small pieces, keep in mind what you would have to get together in the way of prints to carry this out on a full scale. Also, as you hold something small on your worktable, think of the logistics involved in varnishing and sanding a similar piece many, many times as big (Figure 130). Instead of working at a table, you might have to get on a ladder. Instead of raising something up to get at a leg, you might have to practically crawl on your belly.

Third, check your working surroundings. Have you a place where you can work on something large? You can always find a work corner for a box or a tray, but a piano, a commode, or a screen requires a larger area.

Choosing Large Pieces

Finding large pieces presents the least of your problems. As with boxes and plaques, you can either search around second-hand and antique shops for interesting and well-shaped finds, or you can buy unfinished wooden items. Most large department stores have unfinished furniture sections, with styles ranging from traditional to modern.

You might like to try your hand at decoupage on a large scale with a screen. This is a highly useful and designable piece of furniture, yet it is not quite as commonly available as desks and chests of drawers. Many stores do sell inexpensive screens which could be used. You could, as I did,

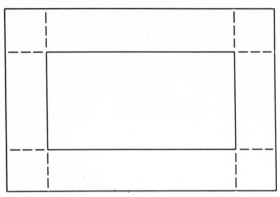

Figure 131. *This diagram illustrates how to make a paper lining for the inside of a box. Cut off the little squares at each corner, as indicated by the broken line. Fold the paper up along the solid lines. The four sides will meet at the edges and the pattern can be glued directly into the box.*

Figure 132. The hand-colored screen is shown in full. (See Color Plate 6.)

search through antique shops until you discover a treasure, or you could make your own screen quite simply and inexpensively with materials from the lumberyard.

My own antique screen required carpentry to make it usable. It came with rather tattered fabric inserts which were replaced with Masonite panels, three panels for each side of the screen.

Since the smooth side of Masonite makes an excellent decoupage surface and since such panels are very lightweight and easy to handle during the long process of painting, designing, varnishing, and sanding, I shall give you instructions for patterning your screen after the illustrated model. Instructions will be for a three-panel screen. You could add panels if you want something larger.

Making Your Own Screen

To make the frame for each panel you will need two 54" pieces of common pine which is 1" thick and 2" wide. For the short side of the frame you will need two pieces 14" long (Figure 131).

The frame could be cemented together with strong epoxy though I prefer hammer and nails. Either way, join at right angles. Half-inch by two-inch brass hinges will be used to connect each of the three frames, three between the first and second frame, three between the second and third frame.

You will need a piece of 16" by 48" Masonite for each panel of your screen. A standard 4' square sheet of Masonite will give you exactly three panels for one side of the screen, eliminating any waste or extra cost. The lumberyard will cut your two sheets into the six panels needed to complete the screen.

While you will not attach your panels to the frame until you have completed your decoupage, make the holes for the screws *before* you start painting and varnishing and be sure to keep these holes free from varnish by passing a toothpick through them now and then. You will need six 3" finishing nails to support each panel. These should be placed about ¼" from each corner, and two will go in the center of the panel, ¼" from the edge.

A finished screen, such as my original model, has some decorative detail on the frame section. This can be easily and inexpensively done when you build your own. Decorative detail will serve to enclose your panels and you will find a wide choice of narrow filigree trims in any lumberyard. They are carved and detailed to suit any type of

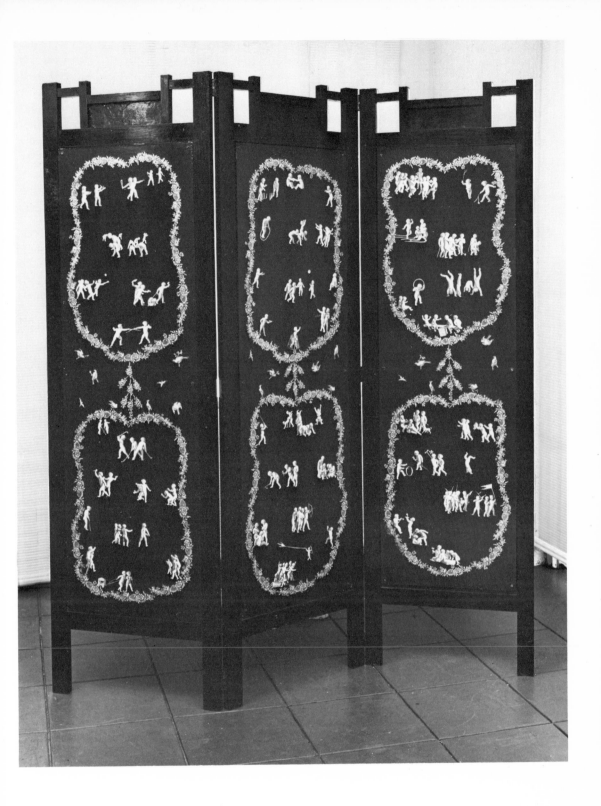

Figure 133. *This is the second side of the Greenaway screen. The theme is still children, but it is a more specific theme of children's games. The whole screen is in black and the prints are almost uncolored. Only a light blue pencil was used in the shadows, with white used to blend the blue, giving a marble look to the finished screen. It is very French and quite elegant.*

Figure 134. Before working on your first large piece, do a piece of doll furniture and think through all the changes involved in making a similar item.

decor. These trims are sold by the foot and if you give your lumberyard the proper dimensions, you can buy your trim pieces cut and mitered at the corners. All you have to do is nail them in place and then paint the trim to match the frame, or in a contrasting color. A little gold or silver leaf finish over the painted surface can be effected by dipping the tip of a cloth into one of the wax finishes such as Rub 'n' Buff.

Large-Piece Design Problems

Whether you decoupage a tiny box or a large screen, the real key to its final artistic success is, of course, the design. With a large piece, this is more important than ever. How do you go about planning your designs? How do you gather together enough to cover a large area?

If you study examples of decorated furniture, be it hand painted or decorated with decoupage, you will find there are two elements always present: theme and repetition.

Theme

Having a central theme for your composition is actually a tremendous aid in planning a design. If you will recall my discussion on design in Chapter 2, I suggested that having a theme is the best possible way to stimulate your thinking towards planning interesting and meaningful compositions. A musical theme, for example, might set you upon a search for pictures of musicians, dancers, instruments, or musical scenes. Once you have the key picture all the other elements fall into place. Everything pertaining to your main theme is placed in a position of prominence. Other design elements such as scrolls and flowers are strategically placed in supporting positions. Thus, the butterflies in my "Kate Greenaway" screen are allowed to flutter along the edges of the thematic stars: the children. The design on the other side of the screen was still based on children, but this time on the more specific idea of children and games. Birds are allowed to fly here and there, but not in such a way as to detract from the main theme of the children and their games.

Repetition Without Rote

All-over or repeat motifs are fine for wallpapers, fabrics, and commercial pottery but not for decoupage. Of course, it takes considerable skill to work out an all-over pattern which is attractive and rhythmic. Once in a while, when using decoupage on furniture, the use of repeat motifs is successful (Figure 116). As a rule, repeat motifs will give you a too perfect and symmetrical look which will emulate the man-made rather than the one-of-a-kind quality which you want for a piece of fine furniture. The aim in handcrafting is to get away from the mass-produced perfection which pervades our everyday lives.

How then, do we get away from this rote repetition of patterns without having a design which rambles all over the place?

First, while you should aim to carry through your main theme with scenes that are *all* different, these scenes should have a uniformity in mood and size scale. When all these diverse scenes are grouped together, they will have the look of a repeat pattern at first glance, so that the viewer is usually delighted to see that each scene tells its own story.

Second, while you will not be likely to take one scene and repeat it, you *can* achieve a *feeling* of repetition and unity by using the same color scheme for all the different scenes. This does not mean that you must color all costumes in identical colors, but you will use *only* a preselected group of colors.

Finally, as long as you maintain diversity in your selection of prints which will express your theme, you *can* use a repeat pattern of identical prints, colored in identical colors, if you use these patterns to unify your main designs. A series of enclosing scrolls are a perfect example of repetition used to unify, without the loss of originality in the main design.

Finding and Choosing Designs

Finding designs to illustrate a favorite theme is really not too difficult. If you are a collector, you might have been gathering pictures of something of special interest to you for months or years. Thanks to the vast array of books offered by publishers, there are likely to be pages and pages of illustrations on any theme. The adorable cherubs at play on the black side of my screen all came from one book on early children's games. Large paperback facsimile books such as *1800 Woodcuts* by Thomas Bewick offer pages and pages of animals and sporting scenes. A similar publication *Catchpenny Prints* features page upon page of figures of old-time tradespeople, hunters, horsemen, comical figures, and family scenes. The

Ladies' Amusement offers many pages of Chinoiserie, strange animals, and insects. These are just a few suggestions. All the materials mentioned are in black and white, suitable for hand coloring. Some of the more unusual, high-quality gift wraps might provide large numbers of either black and white or ready-colored materials.

It is when it comes to finding and choosing a scroll or other repeat pattern to use as an over-all unifier, that you run into the problem of finding a large number of copies of one print. If you choose prints available from a supplier specializing in such prints, you can, of course, buy as many as you need. However, if you prefer something which you have searched out and which you want to use exclusively, you must consider the possibility of making your own print. This is neither difficult nor terribly expensive. Naturally, it would not pay to have a print made up for one small box or picture, but since a large piece of furniture is likely to call for at least twenty or thirty repeats the minimum print order of 100 required by most people doing this type of work does not seem so large.

The printing process you will use is called photo-offset. The material to be reproduced is pasted onto plain white paper, photographed, and then reprinted. Your local classified directory will list at least one or two photo-offset printers. Often a small-town newspaper would provide this service. Prices vary, but the more copies you print, the lower your costs.

Making Your Own Prints

First, choose your material carefully. Only black and white can be reproduced. Line drawings and engravings are ideal. Keep in mind that dark spots will come out darker. Gray will turn black.

Second, cut out what you want and paste it down on a plain white sheet of paper 8½" by 11". Leave a ½" border all around.

The printer can advise you as to whether or not everything you have done will reproduce clearly. That is all there is to it!

Designing a Screen

The basic frame as it was found was in good condition. The fabric inserts were replaced with panels of Masonite, the smooth side to be used for the designs. I decided to stick with the original black of the frame, although the carved sections were highlighted with gold Rub 'n' Buff to give a gold-leaf effect. The panels were painted white which looks rather oriental inside the black frame.

The Prints

The theme of the screen was children; all gay children of the drawings of the nineteenth-century illustrator Kate Greenaway, whose works I collected. (See the Demonstration on prints for a screen at the end of the chapter.) I wanted my screen to be hand colored, so I used only whatever was available in black and white. Since this meant gathering together bits and pieces from many different books with many differently textured papers (many of which would not take to pencils), I had to make up prints not only of my unifying border materials but also of my main scenes.

Once I had all my children gathered together, I still needed something attractive and appropriate to tie it all together. This turned up at a bazaar at a stall where old music was being sold. One music paper had a cover with a marvelous gay-looking scroll which seemed just perfect for my cheerful little boys and girls. The paper was just about falling apart, the scroll would have to be recut to fit an 8½" x 11" print paper, but the designs were clear and in black and white. Since I wanted some small designs scattered all over my screen, I decided to reproduce a whole bunch of my favorite butterflies at the same time I printed up the scroll. (See the Demonstration on preparing prints for reprinting at the end of the chapter.)

The Color Scheme

Although I am a Kate Greenaway admirer, I did want *my* Greenaway children to have colors somewhat brighter than the artist's usually light pastels. Since a great many prints were involved, I wanted a complete and bright range of colors, even though I did not want to confuse my work with *too* many colors. Consequently, I worked out a basic palette which involved ten pencils. I used these ten throughout the screen: terra cotta, dark crimson, soft moss green, strong blue-green, purple-blue, deep red, orange-red, pink, yellow, and white. With these colors I was able to achieve the bright and lively look I wanted and by using them carefully I was able to maintain unity.

To color the children. I used terra cotta in all the shaded areas as an underlay. I shifted my color emphasis from scene to scene. For example, in some scenes the reds predominated, with an accent note of green. In other scenes I let the green and yellow predominate. In still others, I featured blue, with the green as an accent.

To color the enclosing scrolls. I used the ten pencils in exactly the same way in each scroll. Following nature I let the greens predominate, with the reds for my chief accents.

To color the butterflies. I let my colors vary as with the children. Since I had to use some of the butterflies several times, I made certain that no two butterflies were colored the same way.

The Layout

In a big surface such as this, the over-all plan of what you want to do is in your mind as you choose your prints. I knew I wanted my children as a focal point and that I wanted to group them into a series of scenes with the scrolls serving as frames. The butterflies were sort of an afterthought, fluttering into my creative process just as casually as they now flit around the edges of the screen.

When designing it is always a good idea to lay out your complete design on the background to be decorated and then step back to get a good perspective *before* pasting down. With a really large project this is essential. A package of the gumlike, reusable material like Plasti-Tak, Stick-It, etc., is a must (see Suppliers List).

Many decoupeurs who work on large pieces carefully measure and sketch in the spots where their designs will fit so that borders are even to the most minute fraction of an inch. I prefer to work in a looser way, using only my eye as a guideline. The resulting imperfections in layout are compensated for by a freer and more casual look. This is, of course, a matter of personal preference.

Varnishing and Finishing

In varnishing my screen I wanted to keep the colors bright and pure and to minimize the yellowing of the white background under the antique varnish. To prevent yellowing, I put a few drops of cobalt blue from a tube of Universal tinting into each jar of varnish I used. Varnish must always be stirred before using, and with this touch of bluing, a stirring became especially important.

As you varnish your first big piece, you will discover that it takes longer for the designs to sink.

It takes longer than the varnish on a large piece! I cannot really give you a scientific reason for this, but it is so. My screen had more than forty coats of varnish. I did not wait until the last coat of varnish to start sanding. To wait this long to get rid of any imperfections would be disastrous. Sanding was started after the fifteenth coat. I went through the entire sanding process: three grades of wet and dry sandpaper, plus steel-wooling, washing, and drying. Waxing waits until the very end. The sanding and steel-wooling process was repeated every ten coats. I did not really count each and every application, but by the time it was all done, I had completed about three sanding and steel-wooling sessions.

Other Designs

There are several other possible screen designs, some of which are discussed here.

Many scenes. The second side of my screen did not enclose each individual group of children, but had many little scenes placed within one big scroll. This made for a much looser arrangement. When doing two sides of a screen, by the way, it is not necessary to have the two sides tied together in theme or color.

A single design surface. Instead of having each panel an independent unit, the designs may reach across each panel, so that you are working on a single canvas rather than separate but connected ones. The Japanese, famous for their lacquered screens, often have enormous scenes going across four or five wide panels. Keep in mind that by enlarging your canvas from one to several panels you must also increase the dimensions of your designs. In other words, you will need larger figures. The small children on either side of the illustrated screen would have looked undersized and lost had they been used to cover a huge canvas of three abutting panels, without separating scrolls (Figure 135).

Figure 135. Designs can overlap from one panel of furniture to another, instead of having each panel complete in itself.

Papered backgrounds. Paper could add an interesting dimension and unifying note to your screen (Figure 134). Patterned rice papers might be cut and arranged into a mosaic type of background. Or, you might want to arrange your scenes into a series of mosaic pictures using gold papers as frames. (See Chapter 7.)

Three-dimensional techniques. These are not likely to be something you would want to use all over a

151

Figure 136. *At first glance, these tilt-top tables seem to have identical designs. Upon closer inspection you will see that each scene is different. The similarity in the mood of the design and the unifying border designs makes them appear identical.*

screen, but they could work out as accent notes. If you are going to do any experimentation with stuffing and molding prints (as in Chapter 6) you might apply this most effectively to accent and highlight certain prints. For example, a screen with a nature theme would lend itself to having certain animals stuffed and molded.

Whatever your design plan will be, think it through carefully. Take your time. Live with the idea for a while before getting to the final stages. You can't move a screen or a commode into some unobtrusive corner if you're not satisfied with it. It will be there, big and bold, and, if you do it right, it will be *beautiful* too!

Demonstrations

Assembling Prints for a Screen. *Collect together all the materials which will be used for decorating the screen. The materials may come from many sources (as in this case). Notice the many variations in paper textures, some of which could not be colored. Therefore a number of prints had to be made up.*

Preparing Prints for Reprinting. *Often scroll material has to be pasted up for reprinting. Butterflies shown here will be used as accent notes. This scroll was rearranged and reshaped to work around the main scenes of the screen.*

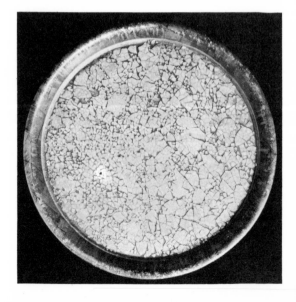

Figure 137. (Above) Here is a full view of a box which has a side border and lining of gift-wrap paper. The top designs are from a book by Dickens. The color scheme was worked around the precolored gift wrap with its hot pink stripe and gold and green lattices. The box background was a soft pink, and the figures are green and gold.

Figure 138. (Right) A tray was completely covered with eggshell inlay. Gold paint was worked into the crevices with a toothpick. Decoupage designs could have been superimposed on the eggshell finish.

14

SPECIAL EFFECTS AND FINISHING TOUCHES

Anything as beautiful as your decoupage deserves tender loving care inside as well as outside. Either paper or fabric linings can be used.

Paper Linings

There are many beautiful papers which are ideal for providing a handsome inside view of a box. Here is an opportunity to use types of paper not suitable for decoupage. For example, wallpaper which is too pulpy and thick to be varnished, or velour-finished papers which would be ruined under varnish, can go with ease inside a box.

Papers which did serve as part of your decoupage can also go inside the box. In fact, the lining can be used to carry through the motif of the outside (Figure 137). The careful decoupeur will, if necessary, recut and reshape even this lining material to achieve the proper spatial relationship. (See the Demonstration on lining a box at the end of the chapter.)

A paper lining can be applied directly to the inside of a box. If your box is round, you simply cut a circle to fit the bottom of the box. The side can be done with one strip. Measure this round side with a cloth measuring tape.

For a square or rectangular box, you can make a pattern for putting the lining in in one piece.

You can use any paste to glue in your paper linings. I found one new product especially helpful in avoiding muss and fuss. This is a waxlike stick which is rubbed over the surface to be glued; the surface then gets sticky and can be pressed down. This is available in all dime stores.

Fabric Linings

Velvets, velveteens, felts, and lightweight quilted fabrics are just some of the materials which make rich and elegant linings. Most of the time you will find it unnecessary to go out to buy materials especially for linings; this is a wonderful opportunity to use up fabric scraps from sewing items or from old clothing which is still in good condition. I have lined boxes with my youngsters' outgrown velour and cotton shirts, old coat linings, and leftover upholstery fabrics.

A fabric lining should not be put directly into a box but should first be glued to a cardboard pattern. To line a box, you will need a cardboard pattern for the bottom and a cardboard pattern for each side. The fabric is cut to overlap, with the corners cut at an angle so that they can be folded down and glued down in back. This prevents any fraying or frizzing (Figures 139, 140, 141, and 142). Be sure to allow for the space to be taken up by fabric. A bulky fabric will take up at least ½" of space, so make sure the cardboard patterns should be cut smaller than the inside proportions of the box. Since fabrics vary so much, you must work this out for yourself according to the texture you have at hand.

While we are on the subject of the insides of boxes, do not forget the backs of plaques and pins and the bottoms of boxes. True, these parts usually remain unseen, but it is something like a finished back which will distinguish the true craftsman.

Signatures

Any artist who takes pride in his work will want to sign it. Since decoupage is a paper art, I feel the signature should be incorporated into the total scheme of things. One of the easiest ways to do this is to use name labels which can then be cut up artistically and incorporated into a part of the top design or glued to the bottom. They can then be

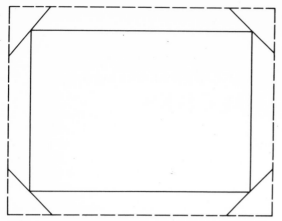

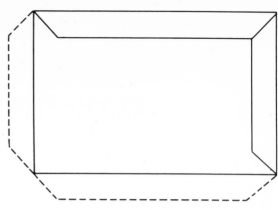

Figure 139. *This illustration and Figures 140, 141, and 142 show how a box is lined with fabric which must first be glued to a cardboard base. Here is the pattern for the bottom of the box lining. The solid lines indicate the size of the cardboard. The broken lines indicate the size of the fabric. The fabric should be cut at each corner as indicated by the solid diagonal lines. This will prevent bunching when the fabric is folded under.*

Figure 140. *This shows the fabric for the box bottom partially folded over and glued down. Note how smoothly the edges meet. The broken lines indicate the fabric still to be folded and glued. The reason for this folding over of the fabric is to avoid frizzing of fabric edges.*

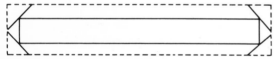

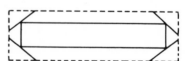

Figure 141. *Here are the pieces needed for the long side of the box lining.*

Figure 142. *These pieces are needed for the short side of the box. The procedure for lining the sides is exactly the same as for the bottom: cut off the corners, fold over the fabric and glue down.*

varnished and rubbed right into the finished work. (See the Demonstration on signatures at the end of the chapter.)

If you prefer your own personalized signature, you could, of course, put your initials into some portion of one of the designs, or cut out a small piece of paper and write your name or initials with a sharp pencil and then paste it into some corner of your design. (See the Demonstration on colored signatures at the end of the chapter.)

Glazing

The reason so many people refer to glazing as antiquing is that a glaze finish does give a painted surface a mellow, antique look. Since the antique varnish you apply to decoupage automatically mellows your colors, glazing is not really essential to decoupage. However, if you want to add color highlights, glazing is an easy and effective way to do this. You can apply glaze right after your paint dries, or wait until you have put on five or six coats of varnish.

Antique glazes are commercially available in all paint stores, but since they are so easy to make up and can be kept in a sealed glass jar indefinitely, let us see what goes into a good glaze and how it would be applied.

Basic Glaze Formula

A glaze is made up of a mixture of three parts turpentine to one part varnish. Into this mixture a glazing color from a tube of oil paint is mixed and squeezed. If this sounds too much like a dab of this and a dab of that recipe, here are specific instructions: mix ¼ cup varnish, ¾ cup turpentine, and ½ teaspoon of linseed oil: into this squeeze 1" from a tube of raw turkey umber (oil paint). (The raw umber is a very popular glazing color. However, you could substitute black sienna, or even blue, red, or green.)

Applying Glaze

Dip a brush or a clean rag (cheesecloth is very good) into your glazing mixture. Wipe or brush it all over your surface. Do not get scared if it all looks like a brown mess, and your beautiful design seems to be obliterated.

After about a minute, take another clean rag and wipe away. It will wipe away with just bits of the color clinging here and there. It is in this wiping away process that you control the amount of color that remains. Rub hard where you want the color removed, gently or not at all where you want it strong. Furniture-finishing people who work with intricately carved surfaces usually allow the glaze to dry up and remain in the carved areas.

If you find that you do not like your glaze, dip a rag into turpentine and wipe the whole thing off. Start again.

Alternative Ways of Glazing

If you work fast, you need not prepare a glazing mixture at all. Just dip the tip of a cloth into turpentine and then into a dab of oil color. Rub the color where you want and wipe away.

You can also glaze with water-based paints. I like this technique myself since it is simple, odorless, and allows lots of control over the color. I squeeze a little acrylic watercolor into a tablespoon or two of water. When this mixture is stirred into a wash, I rub it gently with a cloth over my surface. Clear water will remove any excess color, or, if you want, the whole thing.

Gold Leafing

At one time gold leafing was a complicated art which involved gilding and fine foil. Today, with many gold paints and powders on the market, gold leafing effects can be achieved in the same easy manner in which you glaze. Products like Rub 'n' Buff and Treasure Gold can be applied like wax with a fingertip, cotton swab, or the corner of a rag. I like to moisten a cotton swab with a dab of turpentine for more control.

Gold paint can be used in a gold-leaf effect, too. Just dip a very thin brush lightly into well-stirred gold liquid and rub off with a cloth dampened with turpentine. There are water-based gold paints available, too. Some of these fast gold-leaf finishes are available in silver and other metallic shades.

Inlays

A very interesting background treatment is mother-of-pearl flakes or an eggshell inlay. Both of these are old crafts practiced by fine furniture finishers. The inlays are covered with many coats of antique varnish, sanded, and rubbed exactly like decoupage. The inlays have the same wonderful patina as any decoupage finished design and this is why they combine so well with the craft. Since these inlays have a mosaic appearance, they were mentioned in the chapter on mosaic decoupage (Chapter 7).

Mother-of-Pearl Flakes

Mother-of-pearl is a natural material, an iridescent layer grown inside a shell. One shell yields about three or four small sheets of this iridescent material. Since these pearl sheets are quite brittle, bits and pieces tend to fall away from the larger sheets and these flakes are available from crafts supply stores. A little box of flakes will have all variations of flake shapes and thicknesses. It is best to sort them out before you start on a project. The flakes can be used to make a border around your decoupage designs (Chapter 12) or as a whole background (Chapter 7). The mother-of-pearl flake background will never be as completely smooth as a painted wood finish. However, the iridescent sheen of the flakes more than offsets the slightly bumpy background.

The flakes are somewhat tedious to apply, but the process is not hard. First, sort out the flakes you want and lay them out on wax paper, shiny side up. Apply white glue to the surface to be decorated, coating a small area at a time. Dip a toothpick in water and use this as you would a magnet to pick up your flake and set it into the white glue. Now, allow the flakes to set into the background overnight. After this, sand smooth with dry No. 400 sandpaper.

You can now superimpose your decoupage designs and finish with a clear lacquer finish to maintain the pure sparkle of the flakes.

Eggshell Inlays

Eggshell inlay is applied very much like mother-of-pearl flakes. The ingredients are, of course, right in your refrigerator. The results can be unique. Again, the procedure is simple, but tedious. This is how it is done.

First, soak your eggshell in bleach for a day or so. This will loosen the inner membrane and give you a nice thin shell to work with. I like to use my shells pure white, but you could soak them in vegetable colors and dye them like Easter eggs.

In gluing the shells down, instead of applying glue to the background to be covered, apply a dab of glue to the underside of your eggshell. Work with ½" pieces and lay the eggshell, glue side down, onto your surface. Now, take a pushpin or other pointed tool and crack the shell.

Use the pushpin to move the pieces, which have spread as you cracked them, together again. You are, in effect, creating your own mosaic in the way you crack the shells and move them together. The closer you can get the shells together, the nicer the finish. However, if you paint your background a vivid color, this will show between the mosaic bits, giving the effect of a mosaic grouting.

When the eggshells are all down tight, clean off any excess glue with a swab dipped in vinegar (you do not have to clean off glue in the mother-of-pearl: it works to level spaces). Then, rub with dry No. 400 sandpaper.

Finally, superimpose your designs, and finish with antique varnish or a lacquer-based finish. I like the antique varnish for eggshells, especially the white ones. The patina and shading are just lovely. One of my students covered a tray in eggshell and by the time the job was complete she decided it was beautiful in its pure state. Thus, instead of applying decoupage designs, she used a toothpick to run some gold paint into her cracks. The result is quite magnificent (Figure 138).

Mother-of-Pearl Sheets

If you wish to work with the mother-of-pearl sheets to either underlay or overlay a decoupage design (the pearl sheets are so translucent that your design *will* show through if the pearl is superimposed on the design), you must soak these sheets before they can be cut and glued. The easiest way to handle them is to keep the pearl in a bowl of water. (It can soak for days.) This is exactly the same process used by a manicurist. She soaks your hand in a bowl of warm water so that your nails will soften and can be cut more easily. Since you will be cutting these sheets of pearl with your decoupage scissors to fit a decoupage design, you too will want to soften what you are cutting. Mother-of-pearl is an expensive material and it should also not be overdone in decoupage, so use it sparingly. It serves well to accent a bird's plumage or to highlight a leaf or a petal. An outline drawn on the pearl sheet with pencil will not harm the surface. Since it is very thin, you should have no problem sinking it all down smooth and flat during varnishing.

Rottenstone and Oil

For an extra gloss or piano finish, apply a mixture of rottenstone and oil after you have sanded and steel-wooled, but before you wax. Rottenstone comes in powdered form and is available in hardware stores. Mix it in a disposable plastic lid. A teaspoon of the powder into four teaspoons of oil will go a long way. Apply with a clean cloth in fast, even strokes. Buff immediately and thoroughly, then wax.

Demonstrations

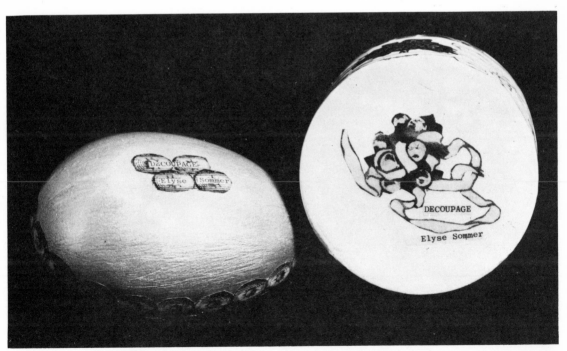

Designing Signatures. *Two examples of how signatures can be worked right into the design. Closeup of the bottom (left) of an egg box. The border motif was used on the bottom of the box, and the name worked right into this motif. The bottom (right) of a small box, with the signature from a label worked into a bit of the scroll used at the sides and top of the box.*

Lining a Box. Here decoupage border design is carried through as a lining. If you look closely at the paper from which the design was taken, you will see that the lining paper was redesigned. To give a better spatial relationship, only the elements used outside the box were included in the lining.

Coloring Signatures. Place the signature on the inside lid of a box, for example, as a part of one of the design motifs. It should then be colored along with the rest of the design.

15

PROBLEMS AND SOLUTIONS

This chapter is dedicated to all my students who have called with varying degrees of desperation to ask, "Something went wrong, what shall I do?" In helping them to work out *their* problems, I have been able to anticipate the ones most likely to be encountered by you. Hopefully, you will never have any mistakes which need correction, but it is a boon to your self-confidence to know what to do—just in case.

Faded Colors

If your colors seemed to fade when you sprayed them, undoubtedly you sprayed too closely and too much. A spray can should be held an arm's length from the subject, and the spray should be lightly applied by moving the can in a circular motion. You want to give your colors a light protective mist of spray, not a drenching. Allow your spray to dry thoroughly and go over your colors, making them deeper than you did before. Now, spray again *carefully*.

Problem Edges

If you start varnishing and an edge pops up, remove the varnish with distilled alcohol if the varnish is still wet. Use your fingernail or a toothpick to lift up the edge as far as it will go. Now, use the toothpick to scrape away whatever varnish has accumulated under the print. Take a fresh toothpick and slip a dab of glue under the edge. Press down and let dry overnight. Clean around the edges to make sure it is really down tight.

Dirt and Varnish

If you dropped your freshly varnished piece and it has become covered with dirt, take a cloth dipped in distilled alcohol and gently clean everything away. You will be removing your last layer of varnish too, but no matter. Wait a day before you varnish again. Do not use turpentine.

Varnish Lumps

Properly stored varnish should not get lumpy. As I mentioned in Chapter 2, it should be kept in small jars to prevent excessive exposure to air. The best place to keep it lump-free is in the refrigerator. If stored in the can, the can should be sealed tight, *hammered* shut, and stored upside down so any scum which does form will at least stay at the bottom.

Once your varnish has become lumpy, however, you need not necessarily throw it out. Here is how to save your varnish: take a plastic spoon and skim the lumps off the top. If it's still lumpy, take an old stocking and strain your varnish through that into a fresh jar.

Shiny Surfaces

If you start varnishing and your surface has an extremely high gloss, something is wrong if you are using a semigloss or eggshell finish. Probably, you did not stir your varnish before you started. If you have applied only one or two coats, do not worry. Stir your varnish each time you use it from now on. If you have already done considerable varnishing, take steel wool and lightly rub off some of the gloss. If a lot of your varnish has already been used, you will never have the right proportions again. It would be best to start a new can.

Problems With Lacquer Finishes

If you have been using a lacquer-based finish, you may find it hard to handle. It may be so thick that it dries before you can move your brush or you may get a lot of hair marks. In fact, lacquer-based finishes *are* stiffer to use; they do not flow onto the finish. To avoid as many problems as possible, keep your brush in lacquer thinner when not in use and leave some of this thinner on your brush before you dip it into your finish. This way, your finish will be thinner and more flexible. You will also find less hairs popping out of your brush.

Varnish Runs

As long as you do not keep varnishing over these runny spots which look like lumpy teardrops, all is not lost. Stop the minute you see a varnish run. You will usually notice them just before you are ready to revarnish. Take No. 600 sandpaper, dry and gently rub out the run. Now, take a tiny piece of No. 0000 steel wool and using circular motions, rub. Clean carefully. Subsequent coats of varnish make the rubbed look in that one spot disappear.

Check the lighting in your work area. Are you varnishing under a good light so you can see varnish runs as they occur?

Varnish Bubbles

The earlier in the game a bubble appears, the easier it is to get rid of. Once your piece has been finished and really hardened, the process of trying to get out a bubble will be more and more risky.

Here is what you do: take a single-edged razor blade and make a slit into the middle of the bubble. Now, gently, *very gently*, use a toothpick to dig out any dried-up varnish. Use a fresh toothpick to slip in fresh glue. A finished piece will have become much more brittle than one still in the works. Thus, while bubbles can be cured, it becomes more and more risky as the piece dries.

Surface Pitmarks

If lots of little pitmarks have crept into your surface during varnishing, this means you have been laying your varnish on too thickly. The little bumps will come out with rubbing. However, if you have lots of them, it is a good idea to start rubbing as soon as your design has sunk in sufficiently to withstand the abrasion.

Rubbing Through to the Paper

If you have rubbed through this much, *stop* rubbing at once. Take a colored pencil close to the color of the design you have rubbed through, a shade darker if possible. Wet the tip of the pencil and touch up the part that has been worn away. Now go back to varnishing, at least two or three coats. Remember that spot when you rub. Skirt it carefully to prevent a recurrence.

Getting Rid of Varnish Bubbles

If your finished piece looks as if it has prickly heat, somehow dampness has been trapped underneath your surface. Take steel wool and erase the wax finish. Rub down with your wet and dry sandpapers. Wash off and dry. Steel-wool again. Apply two to three coats of varnish. Steel-wool, but do not sand. Wax.

Varnish Chips

If your finished piece has been dropped, for example, and there is a chip, take off the finish as you would for the prickly heat situation. Touch up any color that has come off as you would if you had rubbed through. Now, fill in your chip hole with a glob of varnish; a toothpick makes a fine applicator. Repeat this until that chip hole is filled in. Now, give it an over-all coat of varnish. Steel-wool. Do not sand. Wax.

Restoring Finished Decoupage

If it has been a year or so since you completed your decoupage, the edges may seem to be coming out a bit. This can happen, especially if you live in a humid climate. Use your steel wool to rub off the wax finish. Apply two to three coats of varnish. Steel-wool. Rewax.

16

DECOUPAGE AND THE ARTS AND CRAFTS TEACHER

The continuing life of a craft depends not only upon artists who give the public a chance to see their work and develop an appreciation of it but upon teachers who will share their knowledge with those interested in learning to do as well as to view.

When I first became interested in decoupage, very little reference material was available. Art supply and crafts merchants were unfamiliar with the necessary supplies. Lessons from one of the few experts around involved long-distance traveling.

My own decision to teach was born from a need to get away from constant calls to answer the same question: "I've seen your work! It's beautiful. *How* is it done? " If I were going to spend all my time on the phone giving out piecemeal information, I might as well answer questions properly.

When the Lawrence, Long Island, public schools first offered my course as part of their adult program, students fought to get into the class. When the course was offered on the North Shore, in the Great Neck adult program, the classes were immediately filled to the brim.

Both school brochures stressed that this was a course in an old craft requiring great patience. Obviously, twentieth-century craftsmen are *not* too impatient with this or any other old craft.

Fortunately, there are any number of capable and talented people teaching decoupage today. However, as more people are exposed to the beauty of the craft, more and more will want to learn how to do it, and the need for teachers will continue. It is to help those readers who are already experienced and, hopefully, those who will become adept and interested enough to teach, that I offer some suggestions for using this book to set up a decoupage course which will be stimulating to both student and teacher.

Since the need to plan for projects, demonstrations, and materials, and to find ways to bring out the best in each student, is not limited to decoupage, the general arts and crafts teacher might find a number of helpful tips in this chapter.

Teaching Decoupage to Adults

Let us consider a plan for ten two-hour sessions for an adult school or community center program. By skipping certain special projects you can, if necessary, adapt this plan to a shorter program. However, if you find that you must eliminate sessions, do not eliminate the fine hand-colored, eighteenth-century type of decoupage. Students need a good base to have a lasting appreciation of a craft. Once they learn fine cutting, coloring, proper attention to design, and finishing, they can continue to learn on their own. They can work out shortcuts and experiment with easy and quick techniques for themselves, but they will do so without sacrificing sound artistic values, *if* you have instilled them.

It is important to understand the adult student of crafts. Typically, she (women predominate, but there are usually one or two men in each group) will have yearned for a way to express herself artistically, but feels handicapped and insecure because of her inability or unwillingness to draw. Your over-all aim as a teacher then will be to free your students from any of these feelings of inadequacy.

You will be spending a great deal of time teaching the technical skills of the craft, but the real breakthrough in developing a decoupeur will come as the student becomes more concerned with color and designs than with details of the finish. The decoupage finish is beautiful, but one can tire of a finish. A really sound design is never tiresome.

My lesson plans are designed to allow each student to make a number of projects, exploring all sorts of materials, always reinforcing the skills practiced in the first two sessions. Students who have little time or inclination to do work at home can skip some of the projects without feeling left out.

I have broken down each session into three parts. These parts are: first, teacher's materials; second, student's materials; and third, the lesson.

If the school where you teach has a duplicating machine, it is a good idea to have enough copies of this plan made up to hand out at the first session. This will save considerable class time.

Session One

Teacher's materials should consist of books on decoupage, sample materials to give the students an idea of design sources available: *Ladies' Amusement*, paperback books usable for decoupage and available through your local stores, a sample of unfinished crafts items and samples of finished decoupage. At least one pair of decoupage scissors should be available to demonstrate and, ideally, two or three extras should be kept at hand for those who come unprepared. Bring sample cutting materials such as blank paper, pieces from prints you no longer need, magazines. You will also need colored pencils.

Students will need decoupage scissors. Information about what type to bring should be included in the course description.

The first lesson should be an introduction to decoupage (see Chapter 1) and cutting (see the cutting exercises in Chapter 2).

Session Two

The teacher should have colored pencils, a sharpener, and sample materials for coloring.

Students should bring colored pencils, materials to color and cut, and scissors (the latter should be part of the materials the students will bring every week).

The lesson should be on the techniques of coloring and cutting (see Chapter 2).

Session Three

The teacher will need materials to give a demonstration on gluing (see Chapter 2). These materials should include a box containing miscellaneous items such as dry sandpaper, wet and dry sandpaper, jewelry findings, extra crafts items, rags, sponges, glue, pressing roller, wax paper, etc. All these things should from now on be kept on hand for every session.

Students should bring paint, brushes, sandpaper, rags, etc., to do any finishing of box or plaque background in class. If finishing was done at home, materials to color, cut, and plan for designs should be brought.

The lesson involves helping students not familiar with background painting to prepare first projects. Students who did the preparation at home may be helped in the planning of their designs. There should be a class demonstration on how to glue (see Chapters 2 and 3).

Session Four

The teacher should bring samples of under-glass decoupage and materials to demonstrate varnishing.

Students should continue projects in the works plus anything additional they are ready to design so that they will be varnishing several things at once.

The teacher may offer individual help with the designing and pasting down of remaining first projects. Also, students may be instructed in planning additional firsts such as rocks (see Chapter 4), different types of boxes, metal containers, etc. (see Chapters 2 and 3).

Session Five

The teacher should bring samples of acrylic non-rub-finish projects (see Chapter 11) and/or three-dimensional projects (see Chapter 6). The teacher may choose one of these projects or leave the choice to the students. Planning for a session on two levels would let students do either or both of these projects.

Students should bring a glass plate, ashtray, or wide-necked canister. Prints, colored pencils, scissors, gluing materials will also be needed.

The teacher can continue helping students design under-glass projects (see Chapter 11). Students should bring in designs colored, cut, and ready for gluing. The instructor can then give a demonstration on actual decoupage under-glass projects.

Session Six

The teacher should bring in materials and samples to help advanced students plan additional projects. This is a good time to introduce ceramic greenware (see Chapters 8 and 12), rocks (see Chapter 4), photo decoupage (see Chapter 10). The teacher should also bring in finished examples of papier-mâché decoupage (see Chapter 5) or ceramic decoupage (see Chapters 8 and 9), depending upon which subject will be taught.

Students should bring in prints and background for doing quick-finish projects, such as key chain disks, paper sculpture, or other three-dimensional projects.

The lesson can be an explanation and demonstration of processes involved in projects at hand. Work should be done with students on their individual projects.

Session Seven

The teacher's materials can be shared for either a ceramic or papier-mâché session. Bring in some more samples of finished total crafts decoupage items (see Chapters 5 or 8 and 9).

Students should have newspapers, glue, corrugated boards, big scissors, etc., if working on papier-mâché or self-hardening clay with knives. Rolling pins, etc., will be necessary if the students will be working in clay.

The teacher can continue helping students work out their bases. Also, she can lead a discussion of what to do in terms of drying pieces at home. Painting should be explained for those who wish to do this work at home.

Session Eight

The teacher should provide samples of decoupage executed with special finished, linings etc. (see Chapter 14) in preparation for a session on finishing up.

Students' first projects should be ready to bring in for rubbing and sanding in class, reinforcing the original demonstration (see Chapter 2). The handmade background from last week, with designs, should be ready.

In the lesson, review varnishing, rubbing, etc., by supervising students as they apply these techniques to their own finishing projects. Designing the handmade items can be part of the rest of the session.

Session Nine

The teacher should demonstrate the use of materials for linings and special techniques such as mosaic eggshell and mother-of-pearl inlays, and antiquing (see Chapter 14).

Students should bring in work in progress, including anything which needs lining.

The teacher should demonstrate the various special effects and finishes and aid in individual work with students on these demonstration techniques.

Session Ten

The teacher should compile a list of books for further study by students (see Bibliography), a list of suppliers' resources (see Suppliers List).

Students should continue work in progress which needs finishing help and discuss items which they wish to do in the future with the teacher.

The final lesson ought to be a summing up and review. A detailed question and answer session should take up most of this session. Students should be encouraged to exchange addresses so that they will have a chance to meet together after the course ends and thus keep their activity and interest alive. The teacher should review and demonstrate anything students feel unsure of. There should be a discussion of problems past and future. (see Chapter 15) and individual help with planning larger projects (see Chapter 13.)

Note: A teacher who really goes at a fast pace can combine Sessions 9 and 10 and give one class to papier-mâché and one class in ceramic decoupage. However, for most groups this is likely to be too much to absorb and finish in a short time span.

Decoupage for the Sick, Handicapped, or Elderly

Anyone with some special crafts know-how can give joy by sharing this knowledge with the sick, elderly, or handicapped.

Some crafts, of course, cannot be adapted to the limitations of the sick, failing eyesight, and arthritic hands. Many can and decoupage is among them.

Keep in mind the physical limitations of the person or persons you work with, the limitations of the surroundings, the lack of proper work surfaces, small sinks limited to water clean-up and lack of tools and normally available household supplies.

Adapting Decoupage to Special Needs

Several steps in decoupage can be changed or substituted in cases where they may prove to be too strenuous or unwieldy for the shut-in or elderly. Here are some suggestions:

Eliminate varnishing. The person you will be teaching in these special circumstances needs the satisfaction of a project which can be finished fast. Also, varnishing involves brushes, a place to keep or clean them, and sanding, which can be messy and painful for arthritic joints.

Use polymer gloss medium. This is an excellent substitute for varnish (see Chapter 11). It will act as a pasting-down and glazing agent, requires no rubbing, and can be finished in one sitting.

Eliminate background painting. This need not be eliminated in all instances, but when it is not feasible, you can substitute brightly colored gift wraps which can be pasted down as background (see Chapter 3). Design papers should include black and white as well as ready-colored prints.

Emphasize hand coloring. While it is a good idea to shorten the finishing process, hand coloring is very well suited to the sickroom and adds to the sense of creative achievement. Colored pencils are a most necessary supply.

Decoupage for the Handicapped

Plaques and straight-edged boxes can be papered easily. Whenever possible try to relate the craft activity to something which is part of the person's daily life. That way you might help someone adjust to a physical therapy device or a sickroom necessity more positively. For example, a can becomes fun when decoupaged, as do crutches and unattractive slippers and orthopedic footwear. A bedside tray becomes a pleasant reminder of creative activity, rather than a grim reminder of immobility.

Decoupage for the Teacher or Scout Leader

Decoupage is a craft primarily for adults and many teachers do not even consider it as a possibility for children in an arts and crafts program. Yet, the mosaic lesson worked out by Mrs. Selma Feld for her seventh graders (see Chapter 7, Figures 63, 65, and 66) was most satisfying.

The emphasis when working with youngsters must almost always be on design rather than finishes. Some youngsters *will* be intrigued with what they call the real thing and should be given the information needed to pursue this type of finish on their own. For classroom use, polymer gloss is the ideal finish (see Chapter 11).

The use of handmade plaques and boxes of papier-mâché and clay (see Chapters 5, 8, and 9) utilizes materials available to art teachers everywhere. The decoupage designs used to finish off papier-mâché and clay work simply add a new dimension, an interesting bit of history about an old craft, to a basically familiar art lesson. In encouraging the student to work out a total crafts product and in using the paper cutout techniques in a fairly freehand manner, the craft is released from its too tight, too adult aspects. The silhouette-cutting techniques in Chapter 11 would also lend themselves to a lesson.

Using decoupage in conjunction with natural materials such as rocks and driftwood (see Chapter 4) emphasizes an important crafts concept, the utilization of nature for one's own artistic expression. Since scouting programs direct much of their merit badge work towards a knowledge of nature, decoupage on rocks can provide an interesting and novel opportunity to earn a nature badge, and to make Mother's Day and Father's Day gift projects.

Crafts are really an exercise in imagination, ingenuity, and adaptability. The crafts teacher who works with young people can use her own ingenuity in adapting those aspects of decoupage suitable for her group, and eliminating anything which she considers too restrictive or fussy.

SUPPLIERS LIST

Many of the supplies written about in this book are available from your local hardware and paint store, and this reference is made throughout the text. With the popularity of crafts in general and decoupage in particular, many of these same hardware and paint stores have added arts and crafts divisions where special decoupage supplies can be obtained. In addition, there are many crafts and hobby shops and ceramics studios in even the smallest towns, and there seems to be a trend towards more of these coming along. In view of the enormous number of these establishments it would be impossible to be acquainted personally with specifics or list them. Just look through the classified section of your local telephone directory under decoupage, ceramics, crafts, or hobbies and you are almost certain to find at least one place near you where you can browse for supplies and test for service.

Because of possible inaccessibility to stores or your personal preference, this suppliers list is limited to places where you can shop by mail. Catalogs or informational fliers are available from all. Be sure to send the required money when a catalog fee is listed. These fees are necessary to defray the increased rates of printing costs, mailing envelopes, and postage.

Books, Papers, and Prints

This is a very small and specialized list. There are hundreds of book publishers and many of them might have books of interest to you as a decoupeur. To track down other possibilities, browse through your library or local book shop. When you find a publisher carrying books of interest to you, write to that publisher and ask for their catalog which they will be glad to send you. If the publisher's address is not in the book, ask your librarian to help you look it up in a publication called *The Literary Market Place* or in *The Writer's Market.*

Americana Review
725 Dongan Ave.
Scotia, N. Y. 12302

Specialists in inexpensive paperbacks with black-and-white reproductions of various old-fashioned subjects.

Dover Books
131 Varick St.
New York, N. Y. 10014

Museum Books
48 East 43rd St.
New York, N. Y. 10017

Specialists in arts and crafts books. Carry every title from every publisher on every craft—even a facsimile of the *Ladies' Amusement.* (Catalog 35¢)

Publishers Central Bureau
33-20 Hunters Point Ave.
Long Island City, N. Y. 11101

Mail order specialists in book remainders from many publishers. Books no longer "current" but often of great interest to decoupeurs, especially at reduced or "remaindered" prices.

Frederick Warne & Co., Inc.
101 Fifth Ave.
New York, N. Y. 10003

Carries modern, inexpensive editions of such old-time favorite illustrators as Kate Greenaway and Randolph Caldecott.

Ann Barton
Vanity Press
334 West 87th St.
New York, N. Y. 10024

Limited line of very unusual and attractive gift wraps.

Patricia Nimocks Connoisseur Studio, Inc.
P.O. Box 7187
Louisville, Ky. 40207

(Catalog of prints costs $1 and includes other materials)

Elyse Sommer
Box E
Woodmere, N. Y. 11598

(Catalog of prints, 50¢)

Boxes, Plaques, Trays

Colonial Handcraft Trays
Newmarket, Va. 22844

Bare metal trays in the Early American manner.

Jamar, Inc.
379 Knollwood Ave.
Winston-Salem, N.C. 27103

Lok-Box, Inc.
Boxwood Lane R.D. #9
York, Pa. 17402

(Catalog, $1)

O-P Craft Co., Inc.
425 Warren St.
Sandusky, Ohio 44870

(Catalog, 50¢)

Ceramic Bisque

The Pottery Shop
P.O. Box 1007
Bowling Green, Ky. 42101

Bisque ware. Specify your interest in decoupage and they will mark suitable items.

Clays

American Art Clay Co., Inc.
Indianapolis, Ind. 46222

Stewart Clay Co.
133 Mulberry St.
New York, N. Y. 10002

Driftwood

Askia Enterprises
P.O. Box 2568
Eugene, Ore. 97402

Egg Specialties

Hoffman Hatchery
Gratz, Pa. 17030

Goose eggs

Mrs. Kathryn E. Johnson
R.D. #2
Easton, Pa. 18042

Goose eggs (include self addressed, stamped envelope)

O-P Craft Co., (see *Boxes, Plaques, Trays*)

Wooden egg boxes

Taylor House
Corner Bench & Perry Sts.
Galena, Ill. 61036

Eggstands, trims, "Eggers' Gazette" (Catalog, $1)

General Craft Suppliers

The following companies sell materials for *all* crafts. In addition to decoupage boxes and finishes they will be able to furnish some of the auxiliary supplies mentioned in this book; for example, clay, instant papier-mâché, jewelry findings, colored papers, composition board items.

American Handicrafts
Tandy Corporation
1001 Foch St.
Fort Worth, Tex. 76107

This company makes a good lacquer-based finish.

Dick Blick
P.O. Box 1267
Galesburg, Ill. 61401

Economy Handicrafts
47-11 Francis Lewis Blvd.
Flushing, N. Y. 11363

Wholesale prices—i.e., twelve items for the price of ten—to small customers. Do not ignore their craft mats and completely unfinished, to-be-assembled items.

Jewelry Supplies

Jewelart, Inc.
P.O. Box 9
Tarzana, Calif. 91536

(Catalog, 35¢)

Sy Schweitzer & Co., Inc.
P.O. Box 106
Harrison, N. Y. 10528

(Catalog, 25¢)

Both these companies include wonderful instructional articles on jewelry making and handling of findings in their catalogs.

Miscellaneous

Creative Crafts
31 Arch St.
Ramsey, N. J. 07446

Bi-monthly crafts magazine. A good place to find out about new products and new sources.

Federal Smallwares Corp.
366 Fifth Ave.
New York, N. Y. 10001

Miniature furniture (Catalog 25¢)

American Stationery Co., Inc.
Peru, Ind. 46970

Walter Drake and Sons, Inc.
94 Drake Bldg.
Colorado Springs, Col. 80901

Twin Brothers, Inc.
Box 662
St. Louis, Mo. 83101

These three companies are suppliers of signature labels.

BIBLIOGRAPHY

Alexander, Mary Jean, *Handbook of Decorative Design and Ornament.* Tudor, New York, 1965.

Anderson, Mildred, *Original Creations from Papier-Mâché.* Sterling, New York, 1967.

Betts, Victoria B., *Exploring Papier-Mâché.* Davis Mass, Worcester, Massachusetts, 1966.

Bread Dough Artistry. Hazel Pearson Handicrafts, 1968.

Browning, Elizabeth Lowry, *With Love and Elbow Grease.* Simon and Schuster, New York, 1968.

Crawford, John, *Introducing Jewelry Making.* Watson-Guptill Publications, New York, 1969

Frégnac, Claude, *Jewelry From Renaissance to Art Nouveau.* G. P. Putnam's Sons, New York, 1965.

Gentille, Thomas, *Step-by-Step Jewelry.* Golden Press, New York, 1968.

Grotz, George, *The Furniture Doctor.* Doubleday, New York, 1962.

Guido, Gregonetto, *Jewelry Through the Ages.* American Heritage, New York, 1969.

Harrower, Dorothy, *Decoupage—A Limitless World of Decoration,* Barrows & Co., West Caldwell, New Jersey, 1958.

Honour, Hugh, *Chinoiserie—A Vision of Cathay.* E. P. Dutton, New York, 1961.

Hunt, Peter, *How To Do It Book.* Prentice-Hall, Englewood Cliffs, New Jersey, 1952.

Hutton, Helen, *Mosaic Making.* Van Nostrand Reinhold, New York, 1966.

Kenny, Carla, and Kenny, John, *The Art of Papier-Mâché.* Chilton, Philadelphia, 1949.

Kuykendall, Karen, *Art and Design in Papier-Mâché.* Hearthside Press, New York, 1968.

Ladies' Amusement or the Whole Art of Japanning. Ceramic Book Co., Newport, Monmouth, Wales, 1959. Facsimile of original published by Robert Sayer in 1752.

Lovoos, Janice, and Paramore, Felice, *Modern Mosaic Techniques.* Watson-Guptill Publications, New York, 1968.

Manning, Hiram, *Manning on Decoupage.* Hearthside Press, New York, 1969.

Meyer, Franz Sales, *Handbook of Ornament,* Dover, New York, 1957.

Moseley, S., et al., *Crafts Design.* Wadsworth, Belmont, California, 1962.

Nimocks, Patricia, *Decoupage.* Scribner's, New York, 1968.

Snowman, A. Kenneth, *The Art of Carl Fabergé.* Boston Book and Art Shop, Boston, Massachusetts, 1952.

Trevor, Henry, *Pottery Step-by-Step.* Watson-Guptill Publications, New York, 1966.

Vanderbilt, Gloria, *The Gloria Vanderbilt Book of Collage.* Van Nostrand Reinhold, New York, 1970.

Wing, Frances S., *The Complete Book of Decoupage.* Coward-McCann, New York, 1965.

GLOSSARY

Acrylics. Plastic-based paints and mediums, water-soluble during use, but nonsoluble and permanent once dry.

Bewick, Thomas. A renowned eighteenth-century wood engraver. He trained many pupils in his Newcastle, England, shop and their combined work is known as that of the Bewick School.

Bisque Ware. Clay which has been fired once in a ceramic kiln. Pronounced "bisk," also known as biscuit ware. Bisque ware is not waterproof.

Bread Dough. A claylike mixture of bread and glue or bread-making ingredients used to make small sculptures and to mend and repair. Hardens by air drying. May be mixed with color before use, or painted after hardening, and coated with glaze.

Cartouche. A French word, derived from the Italian *cartoccio,* meaning a roll or twist of paper. In context of decorative design it is an ornamental enclosure, usually oval or oblong in shape.

Ceramic Decoupage. The use of nonfiring stains or paints and decoupage designs and finish to decorate either bisque-fired ceramics or handmade ceramics. This eliminates the ceramist's use of glazes.

Ceramic Repoussé. A method of achieving a raised effect in an decoupage design on a handmade clay base, by means of working a clay patty or stuffing into the background design. The paper design is molded over this clay patty.

Chinoiserie. A style of ornamentation popular in eighteenth-century Europe, characterized by intricate patterns and an extensive use of Chinese motifs.

Clay, Self-Hardening. A plastic type of clay which requires no kiln firing to harden.

Collage. The product of pasting or gluing paper, cloth, and other materials into pictures or objects.

Decal (Decalcomania). A design on paper especially prepared so that a picture can be transferred to wood, metal, china, or glass. No coloring or redesigning is involved.

Decoupage. The art of cutting out parts of pictures and combining them into an original and pleasing design. The designs are sunk into layers of varnish and sanded and rubbed for a smooth, hand-painted look and feel.

Decoupeur. One who practices the art of decoupage.

Eggshell Inlay. A mosaic design created with broken bits of eggshell. The eggshell pieces are applied to the background with glue, cracked with a pointed tool, and, like decoupage, sunk into many coats of varnish.

Facsimile. An exact copy, as of a book, painting, or manuscript. Facsimile publishers specialize in reproducing rare editions of books otherwise not available to the general public.

Findings. The mechanical fittings used to attach various portions of jewelry so that they can be worn.

Gaze Motion. An optical effect by which the artist guides the viewer's eye to focus on the leading element of the design.

Gesso Acrylic. A ready to use painting ground which acts as a sealer and painting surface for oils, watercolors, or acrylics. Gesso may be mixed with water or other acrylic colors and used as a paint.

Glaze. A finishing coat over painted objects to soften, blend, and mellow. Usually a thinned varnish, tinted with different oil colors from tubes. Water-based paints may be used.

Gloss Medium. An acrylic polymer latex vehicle which acts as a strong adhesive and a crystal-clear textured varnish. It is water-soluble while wet and nonsoluble when dry.

Godey Print. Name given to prints of fashionable ladies and children reproduced from the popular nineteenth-century American magazine, *Godey's Lady's Book.*

Gold Paper Braid. Foil paper embossed with design motifs, especially useful as borders on boxes.

Greenaway, Kate. Nineteenth-century English children's book illustrator. Her gaily clothed children changed the fashion look of Victorian children. Her drawings are collectors' items.

Instant Papier-Mâché. A substance made of pulped paper which, when mixed with water, forms a claylike mixture. It dries rock hard and may be rasped or sanded. Known by such trade names as Shreddi-Mix and Celluclay.

Ladies' Amusement. A book, printed in London in 1752 by Robert Sayer, containing drawings for the cutting and decoupage pleasure of English and French ladies. The full title is *Ladies' Amusement, or the Whole Art of Japanning Made Easy.*

Layered Mâché. Evenly cut and measured layers of paper dipped in glue and pressed together to form various paper-mâché objects.

Montage. Process of combining pictorial elements so that they are both distinct and blended into an over-all artistic production.

Mosaic. A picture or decoration made of small pieces of inlaid stone, glass, paper, etc.

Mosaic Decoupage. A decoupage design created with cut pieces of paper, using either cut colored papers or cut bits and pieces of predesigned prints.

Mother-of-Pearl. A hard iridescent substance which forms the inner layer of certain shells, as that of the oyster and nacre.

Mother-of-Pearl Flakes. Iridescent bits of pearl from soft mollusk shells, useful as border and background decorations in decoupage.

Papier-Mâché. Cut or torn strips of paper mixed with glue and pressed together when moist to form various articles. Strong and durable when hard, papier-mâché may be used in decoupage for making bases.

Paper Sculpture (Papier Tole). Method of creating a three-dimensional effect with two duplicate prints. One print is used as a background, the second one has portions to be raised up, cut out, and sculptured up over a clear hardening glue.

Photo Decoupage. Art of combining photographs with cut and colored decoupage designs. This may be used on any type of background.

Photocopying. Method of reproducing printed material with Xeroxing machines.

Photo Offset. A process of reproducing black and white prints.

Pillement, Jean. Eighteenth-century French artist noted for his gay fantasy flowers, animals, and scenes in the Chinoiserie manner.

Polymer Gloss Medium. See *Gloss Medium.*

Repoussé. A design raised in relief. In decoupage this is achieved by means of stuffing and molding prints.

Rock Decoupage. Art of decorating stones with decoupage.

Sayer, Robert. Eighteenth-century London printer, known to decoupeurs for producing *Ladies' Amusement.*

Scroll. An ornament resembling a spiral or coiled form.

Sealer. In decoupage, sealers are vital to preserve colors of prints. They can be plastic spray or brush-on mixtures of half shellac-half alcohol.

Silhouette. An outline design usually cut out of a black paper, either a single or a folded sheet.

Silicone Sealer. A polymer-type of adhesive used in decoupage for the paper sculpturing technique.

Slab Building. A method of building clay objects by rolling out even slabs of clay and welding them together.

Slip. Clay mixed with water to create a cementing mixture.

Trompe l'oeil. A visual deception in art; literally means to "fool the eye."

Xeroxing. See *Photocopying.*

INDEX

Edited by Heather Meredith-Owens
Designed by James Craig and Robert Fillie
Set in 10 Point Press Roman by J. D. Computer Type, Inc.
Printed and bound in Japan by Toppan Printing Company, Ltd.